STRANGE
and
OBSCURE STORIES
of the
REVOLUTIONARY WAR

By Tim Rowland

SKYHORSE PUBLISHING

Skyhorse Publishing books may be purchased in bulk at special discounts for sales promotion, corporate gifts, fund-raising, or educational purposes. Special editions can also be created to specifications. For details, contact the Special Sales Department, Skyhorse Publishing, 307 West 36th Street, 11th Floor, New York, NY 10018 or info@skyhorsepublishing.com.

Skyhorse® and Skyhorse Publishing® are registered trademarks of Skyhorse Publishing, Inc.®, a Delaware corporation.

Visit our website at www.skyhorsepublishing.com.

10 9 8 7 6 5 4 3 2 1

Library of Congress Cataloging-in-Publication Data is available on file.

Cover design by Jane Sheppard

Print ISBN: 978-1-63450-360-0
Ebook ISBN: 978-1-63450-972-5

Printed in the United States of America

Table of Contents

Preface

Perhaps because of the complexities of modern war, it's fashionable, maybe even comforting, to oversimplify the American Revolution. Yet the Revolution was every inch the sort of geopolitical calliope that we try to make sense of today. Today's Middle East has nothing on eighteenth-century Europe and its colonies for violence, atrocities, intrigue, and thorny alliances, where a thicket of ancient hatreds and grudges were virtually impossible to decipher. Many residents of Britain would have had no clue what it was that those hot-heads in America were trying to prove—by their thinking, the colonists had it pretty sweet, allowed for the most part to pursue their own interests with little responsibility to the parent country under whose protection they operated. Many colonists themselves wondered the same thing (even if they felt no particular love for the Crown), rolling their eyes at the gasbags in the cities with their gibberish about liberty, death, and all.

In fact, a great swath of settlers bottled up on the Atlantic side of the Appalachian Mountains believed not that the British were too authoritative, but that they weren't authoritative enough. These pioneers would have seen little distinction between an ISIS beheading and an Iroquois scalping, and as the Indians, with cause, clutched desperately to their native lands, settlers were aghast that the British did not do more to protect them against such terrorism.

British statesmen in 1775 did know they had a frisky colt on the end of the line, and had been debating for fifty years or better if and when the colonies would break free. America wasn't some contained, controllable sugar island; this was a vibrant, pounding, liquor-fueled mob of opportunists that was encouraged by dreams of fortunes to be had, especially if the prim British spoilsports could be forced to let go of the reins. Visionaries in Britain understood that to hold onto the colony would require a delicate if not impossible balancing act. Already, America had nearly two centuries of European presence under her belt and nurtured a population that for the most part had come to her shores because of one spite or another they held against the Old World. Once these colonists became economically and martially self-sufficient, Britain would cease to be anything beyond a bothersome bureaucracy in need of purging.

So, to maintain the colonists' dependency on the motherland, the British tightened trade and police power, which ironically were the two things most likely to inspire colonists to seek their independence all the more. Out of this were born the cocked-hatted and buckle-shoed buzzwords with which we are all so familiar: Liberty, freedom and representation, pursuit of happiness, and natural rights of man. Every school child knows that tyranny finally transgressed the bounds of what a reasonable man should have to endure, and we burst from an oppressive cocoon to follow the shining light of freedom. We celebrate all this, the birth of a great republic, today, as we should.

But there is so much more to the story that is missed when we stop there. When history is sanitized and spit-polished in the name of creating a national creation story, many interesting people and stories are overlooked because they don't fit neatly into the narrative.

The intention of this book is to add, at least to a small degree, some stories that have fallen out of the mainstream of literature about the Revolution, and perhaps contribute a greater understanding or context to the war in the process. It's not a collection of trivia or in any way an effort to fill in any significant number of blanks. Its purpose is to be educational and fun, while demonstrating that there was a lot more to the Revolution than Washington crossing the Delaware.

Very loosely, this book shadows the chronology of the Revolution proper, which effectively began with the conclusion of the French and Indian War (1763); gained momentum through events that included increasing taxation, the Boston Massacre (1770), and the Boston Tea Party (1773); and then broke into open warfare that, greatly simplified, included the Battles of Lexington and Concord (April 1775), the capture of Fort Ticonderoga (May 1775), the Battle of Bunker Hill and the siege of Boston (June 1775), Washington's defeat and withdrawal from New York (August 1776), the Battle of Trenton (December 1776), Burgoyne's surrender at Saratoga and the entry of France into the war (October 1777), Howe's capture of Philadelphia and the winter at Valley Forge (1777–78), the British capture of Charleston, South Carolina, and invasion of the South (1780), and the British surrender at Yorktown (1781).

Finally, this book is told more from a storyteller's perspective than that of a seasoned historian. It goes without saying that 250-year-old events are often difficult if not impossible to verify. Historians correctly shy away from stories for which there is no proof. Yet many legends told over the years are equally impossible to disprove, and in reality are seldom entirely made up out of whole cloth. Yes, they will generally be "improved upon" with the retelling over the years, some to the point that they become a bit silly and categorically unbelievable. It's worth considering, though, that for every legend that didn't happen, there are a dozen more, far better stories that have been forgotten.

The view here is that, for example, the Molly Pitcher legend, which wasn't firmed up until nearly a century after the war, is worth presenting, even if in standard form it's a bit too perfect. (Molly Pitcher was the moniker awarded the loving wife who followed her husband into battle, took his place at the cannon when he fell, and carried water for parched patriots at the Battle of Monmouth.) But it seems safe to say that if this legend didn't happen exactly as we have been told, something like it did. Molly Pitcher more likely is a composite of several women, including perhaps a profane, whiskey-swilling camp follower picturesquely known as Dirty Kate, who shall we say put a charge into a lot more than cannons, and eventually died of syphilis.

So, in the retelling, we have actually made the story somewhat more heroic and somewhat less interesting. The same might be said for the war itself. It is good that we preserve our idealized creation story; all nations do. It is from this that we draw pride and inspiration. But it is equally rewarding, and more entertaining, when we dig a little deeper beneath the surface.

CHAPTER 1

The War That Started It All

On July 26, 1764, a year after the conclusion of the French and Indian War, and just over a decade before the first shot of the American Revolution was heard the world around, a young teacher named Enoch Brown rang the bell in a one-room schoolhouse where he taught the children of Scots-Irish farmers in south-central Pennsylvania. The school was near the present-day town of Mercersburg, in a broad, fertile valley flanked by long, sleepy blue ridges. On this summer day, Brown wasn't attracting as many takers as usual, but two girls and nine boys grudgingly straggled into the school and took their seats. Brown had barely started the lesson when he heard a commotion and looked up to see four Delaware Indians rushing the door. Having lived on the American frontier long enough to know what was about to happen, Brown dropped to his knees and begged the braves to kill him and spare the children. The Indians accommodated his first wish, but not the second. Several hours later a passerby discovered the bodies of the teacher and ten children, all of whom had been toma-hawked and scalped. The eleventh child, a boy, survived the scalping, and although he lived into old age, he was never right, and he was a walking reminder of grudges long-held. Nineteenth-century historian Francis Parkman called the trag-edy "an outrage unmatched in fiendish atrocity through all the annals of the war."

The war he spoke of was not the Revolution, but the French and Indian War, or Seven Years' War as it was known in Europe. It was, in retrospect, the kindling that lit the Revolutionary fires, having been fought between the years of 1754 and 1763, ending a scant six years before the Boston Massacre. This explosive world war, which would spread to three continents, was started by none other than George Washington (apolo-gists stress that he was only trying to help), who was sent to the frontier by Virginia Governor Robert Dinwiddie to look out for British interests.

In 1755, British General Edward Braddock marched through
the wilderness to drive the French and Indians out of contested
lands over the Allegheny Mountains. Instead, his army was
routed, and colonists who were settling the Allegheny foothills
lost their protection from Indian attack. This dereliction of
duty, as the settlers saw it, led to uprisings against the crown and
ultimately caused rural people to sympathize with the patriots
in the northeastern cities who were agitating for independence.
Courtesy Library of Congress.

The British were pushing into the Midwest—present-day
Ohio and western Pennsylvania—from the east and south,
while the French were pushing into the same territory from the
north and west. The Indians were squeezed from both sides,
but they sided with the French because the French treated
them with respect, while the British treated them like dirt. In
the summer of 1774, Washington's men ambushed and killed
a dozen Frenchmen that they really shouldn't have, and provoked a French attack that led to Washington's surrender, the

only time in the great general's history that he would do so. Washington and his men stoically limped back to Virginia, taunted and robbed by the Indians for much of the way.

The British and colonial Americans, though losing the battle, would win the war. The French were humiliated the world around, an embarrassment they would not soon forget. And while the British had now rousted the French out of North America, they were not gracious in victory, spreading seeds of discontent among enemy and friend alike.

Galling as the Enoch Brown massacre was, settlers soon had reason to be outraged with the British army as well, a force that was supposed to be protecting them from Indian attack, residual hostilities of the Seven Years' War. Tension between the settlers and the government already existed in the mid-Atlantic, following the royal Proclamation Line of 1763, an arbitrary line on a map that largely prevented settlement in the western lands just taken from the French. Colonial militia, which included plenty of frontier settlers, had helped win the war, and now they were being told that they were not entitled to the spoils. For the Scots-Irish, this smelled a lot like the land overbearance that had driven them away from the auld sod to begin with. Worse, when Pennsylvania lifted a trade ban following the cessation of hostilities, the settlers learned that British-sanctioned merchants were sending contraband to the Indians including rum, gunpowder, and even scalping knives. This was an element of free enterprise that was understandably hard for the frontier pioneers, who were attached to their scalps in more ways than one, to appreciate. At the heart of the controversy in south-central Pennsylvania was an Irish-born merchant, land speculator, and Indian agent named George

Croghan, who arrived in the colonies in 1741. Where many settlers saw only brutal, Native American savages, Croghan saw economic opportunity. He began his commercial life as a fur trader and soon was opening up something like a chain of frontier convenience stores at Indian villages, which undercut the British mega-marts that the redcoats had erected for their own utility on major wagon roads. Where the British and the settlers disdained and feared the Indians, the canny Croghan learned their languages and customs, including the routine of gift-giving, which as customs go was the Native American version of basic hospitality.

Croghan lost his shirt during the French and Indian War, when trade with the enemy was prohibited. Even after the war, Indians continued to take out their frustrations over decades of poor treatment at the hands of the Europeans by streaking down out the Appalachian Mountains and laying waste to random farms and settlements from Maine to the Carolinas. Hundreds of settlers in lonely hills and hollows on the eastern edge of the mountains were killed or kidnapped. A farmer looking up from his plow to see a column of smoke over the next ridge would feel a bolt of terror, knowing that the Indians had just killed his neighbors, and he would likely be next.

While the Indian response was brutal, it was not without provocation. Waves of Scots-Irish escaping the tyranny of the Old World had heedlessly spilled across boundary lines established by treaties, lines that had been unfairly drawn in the Europeans' favor to begin with. The Indian tribes of the Northeast were surprised and offended at the uncouth immigrants from the British Isles, and as they regrouped in the

Ohio territories, they correctly predicted that the Appalachian Mountains, in the end, would not be enough to stop the white settlers' encroachment. After the surrender of the French, the Indians gave it one last try in 1763 under the leadership of an Ottowan chief named Pontiac. The uprising was rather quickly snuffed out, but not before the four Delaware braves paid a visit to Enoch Brown's school.

When the dust settled from Pontiac's War, George Croghan was anxious to earn back some of the profits he'd lost during the hostilities, and he wasn't terribly sympathetic to the settlers who had interrupted his commerce. Or at least he felt no qualms selling liquor and weapons—what could go wrong?— to the still-stewing Indians. The Mercersburg settlements (which would include the birthplace of future President James Buchanan) cried foul and petitioned the British authorities to stop the illegal trade. The British, however, were still testy that, while other colonies raised militia to help fight the war, the pacifist Quakers entrenched in the Pennsylvania assembly had refused. Nor were they particularly excited about helping the Scots-Irish, who were in America to begin with to escape His Majesty's rule.

Further, Croghan had cut a deal with British General Thomas Gage to patch things up with the Indians west of the Appalachians. The trader would take a wagon train over the mountains, laden with gifts for the Indians in the Ohio and Illinois territories, greasing some palms and laying the groundwork for British occupation in the west. What Croghan neglected to mention to the general was that the bulk of his wagon train would be stuffed with private goods that he intended to trade to the Indians for furs at a significant profit for himself.

In the mountains there is a saying that to escape notice, "fat possums travel at night." Croghan's mule train, eighty-one animals strong, was a classic fat possum. It would do no good to let the British see his expansive convoy, which obviously packed in a lot more goods than the ceremonial presents that it was authorized to convey. So Robert Callender, a partner of Croghan, who was leading the expedition on March 5, 1765, ducked British authorities by avoiding the main wagon road to Pittsburgh. Instead, he stuck to local trails and deer paths. This sleight of hand might have fooled the British, but the settlers immediately smelled a rat. They tried to reason with Callender, arguing that they themselves would likely be the victims of the incendiary products that Croghan was sending into the arms of their enemies.

Callender did not consider this to be his problem. His ample train ignored the pioneers' pleas and continued its journey west to the foot of a two-thousand-foot-long ridge known as Sideling Hill. Suddenly, a dozen frontier farmers stepped into the path, their faces painted black in a fashion that today would probably strike us as more comical than fierce. But Callender did not find the situation humorous, and readily complied when settlers demanded he and his men unload the horses and place the goods in a pile. The Black Boys, as they came to be known, picked through the goods, taking what was considered useful and burning the rest.

Where Callender had avoided the British regulars before, he now sought them out. He and his men hightailed to the nine-year-old Fort Loudoun, an unconvincing stronghold that for some reason had been constructed in a depression along the Forbes Road to western Pennsylvania. Ironically, it was this outpost that Callender had probably been trying to avoid in the first place, much as an overloaded trucker seeks to dodge Interstate scales. Now, however, Callender burst into the fort and reported the atrocity on Sideling Hill to the Fort Loudoun commander, Lieutenant Charles Grant, a well-meaning young man who was a week shy of his twenty-fifth birthday. Grant's company was tasked with ensuring that the colonial settlers stayed on their own side of the Allegheny Mountains and did not cross over into Indian territory. This would put the British detachment somewhat at odds with the pioneers, who were disinclined to stay put. There was one other card in play, which would have worked in the traders' favor over the settlers: Grant had been taken prisoner by Wyandot Indians near Detroit five years prior, and his release had been secured by none other than George Croghan.

Grant sent a detachment of soldiers to the scene of the crime, where they found some of the Black Boys lounging around in blankets that had probably been rescued from the ensuing bonfire. The British Highlanders chased the Black Boys into the woods, managing to catch two of them. Hustling their captives back to the fort, the soldiers were suddenly blindsided by fifty rifle-brandishing Black Boys, who demanded the prisoners be released. The Highlanders' leader was in no mood to be bullied by a group of frontier ruffians, and his men grabbed four more prisoners, as the Black Boys—not quite ready to take hostilities to the next level—scattered into the forest. Three days later, however, they were back, occupying the high ground overlooking the rickety Fort Loudoun. Grant barred the doors, manned the shooting decks, and sent out a messenger demanding to know who would have the audacity to menace "the King's fort." James Smith, a respected settler who in a past life had spent a considerable amount of time as a captive of the Indians and was the Black Boys' leader, stepped forward and demanded that the redcoats release his men. If the British refused, the colonial settlers were prepared to fight and die for their cause.

Grant hesitated. A firefight was risky, since he was significantly outnumbered and the fort was not terribly secure. But a representative of the Crown could hardly submit to rabble—the precedent and embarrassment were too terrible to think about. Grant attempted to gather reinforcements by sending messengers to Fort Bedford, forty miles to the west. But the Black Boys captured one messenger after another, until Smith had more prisoners than Grant. Both sides were somewhat flummoxed until Callender solved the standoff by offering to post bail for the colonial prisoners, whom Grant then released. But he kept their guns. This proved an unwise move, because on the frontier at that point in time, the muskets might have been somewhat more valued than the men pulling the trigger. The Black Boys would eventually return for the weapons, and if it meant attacking an official British fort to get them, then that's exactly what they'd do.

Back in Philadelphia, word of the uprising against the Crown created no small amount of consternation. Croghan had acted illegally, it was true, but the settlers had directly flaunted British authority. In a case such as this, where the issue was difficult to sort out, the government fell back on what it did best—nothing. Meanwhile, wealthy capitalists, and people hoping to become wealthy capitalists, were angry over the Proclamation Line as well, for reasons that weren't all that different from the farmers'. While not amused by the thought of armed, lawless clodhoppers on the frontier burning loads of freight, in the end they also wanted the newly won English lands to be open to trade and speculation.

This was an important moment in the history of the American Revolution. For perhaps the first time, everyone in colonial America—rich and poor, urban and rural—wanted the same thing: the spoils of the French and Indian War. And it was the King who was standing in the way. Historian David Dixon wrote, "British officials could not know when they first concocted the Proclamation Line that the measure would help to make colonial America a crucible in which resentful and defiant social strata would come together. Within this cauldron of discontent can be found the ingredients for revolutionary agitation."

The only thing lacking for an all-out rebellion at the moment was gunfire. It wouldn't be lacking for long. The aggrieved settlers took Philadelphia's indecision as license to establish their own highway patrol, notifying convoy drivers hauling goods to the west that their loads were subject to inspection and required a pass from the local magistrate. Those who failed to obtain a pass were roughed up, even if they were legitimately hauling goods to restock military forts. On May 6, 1765, the uncooperative crew of a packhorse train was bound and beaten near a residence picturesquely known as Widow Barr's Place. This time Lieutenant Grant sent soldiers out from the fort to confront the Black Boys, and the two sides set pleasantries aside and actually began firing their weapons at each other—somewhat ineffectively, as the only injury was suffered by a settler named James Brown, who was shot in the leg.

This tentative fighting continued through the summer and fall until the Black Boys, who couldn't stop thinking about those guns that Grant had refused to return, brought a force 300 strong to attack Fort Loudoun. Badly outnumbered, Grant gave back the eight rifles in question, and shortly afterward the British regulars gave up their fight against the Black Boys and abandoned the fort.

The Black Boys Rebellion is seldom remarked upon today, probably because it produced only the one minor casualty. But for nine months the two sides had slung lead at each other, even if the results had been unimpressive. In fact, it would seem that the safest place to be in all of colonial America at the time was standing in opposition to the enemy's guns. However, the action was still significant because at no point in the skirmishes would the Black Boys or the British regulators have considered themselves to be safe from harm. Both sides were serious. At one point Lieutenant Grant, out for a walk, was captured by the Black Boys and tied to a tree. Had any one of the Black Boys impulsively swung a rifle butt or pulled a trigger (and they had certainly made threats that they were willing to do so) the British army likely would have fallen on the Black Boys in force and a full-fledged war would have broken out. At this particular time, some of the more egregious British tax policies had yet to be introduced, so the colonies as a whole weren't the tinderbox they would become in 1775—but the Pennsylvania colonists felt just as aggrieved as the Massachusetts colonists did at Lexington and Concord ten years hence.

As it was, some historians are loath to even call the Black Boys action a rebellion, because the settlers basically just wanted the British to enforce the law. But Lieutenant Grant referred to it as a rebellion, and Black Boys leader James Smith considered himself and his men to be rebels. Perhaps both were overstating things. The Black Boys, after all, didn't want to throw off the yoke of government; they wanted the government to do its job. Still, it's difficult to conclude that the settlers were not at root rebelling against British authority. If issuing commercial permits, seizing and destroying property, and shooting against a standing army was not a rebellion, it was doing a relatively credible impression of one.

Nor was the Black Boys Rebellion entirely unique. There were at least a half-dozen other uprisings against authority in the century before Lexington and Concord, where colonists resorted to violence. In 1676, Bacon's Rebellion broke out when Nathaniel Bacon led several hundred Virginians against the unpopular colonial Governor William Berkeley, whom they viewed as too conciliatory toward the Native Americans. The mob chased Berkeley out of the capital and burned Jamestown to the ground. Things might have gotten interesting except for the untimely death of Bacon a month later. Without the charismatic Bacon to gin them up (literally and figuratively), the rebels quickly lost interest in the face of governmental pushback.

A year before the Black Boys Rebellion, the Paxton Boys—a militia of maybe 250 Scots-Irish settlers organized by the Reverend John Elder, parson of a church in Paxtang, Pennsylvania—marched on Philadelphia, demanding revenge against the Indians for raids conducted during Pontiac's War. The angry mob was talked off the ledge by a group of city fathers, including a man by the name of Ben Franklin.

In the long view of history, however, these events seem less like rebellions than psychotic episodes. Bacon, charitably described by historians as "complex," and Berkeley had a florid hatred of each other that drove the violence. At one point, Bacon and his men leveled their guns at Berkeley, demanding that the governor authorize Bacon to lead militia against the Indians. Not only did Berkeley refuse, the seventy-one-year-old governor ripped open his shirtfront and screamed for Bacon to go ahead and shoot if he had the guts. The rebels thought it over for a moment before turning their weapons away from Berkeley and toward a number of colonial lawmakers gathered nearby, who immediately granted Bacon his desired commission.

The Paxton Boys had the same issues as the Black Boys, but instead of taking their fight to the government, they made an ignominious name for themselves initially by slaughtering twenty peaceful members of a local Susquehannock Indian tribe that had no connection with the raiders from the west. Although the Reverend Elder was not complicit in this attack, his philosophy certainly set a tone. Known as the "Fighting Parson," he, like many Presbyterian Scots-Irish ministers in the middle colonies, preached with a gun leaning against the pulpit.

The commonality of these and other uprisings prior to the Revolution—and the reason they are important—was the involvement of lower classes. Farmers aggrieved at both the Indian attacks and governments that did not seem to care if they lived or died were now on the same page as merchants and planters, who had their own financial reasons for breaking free of the British. Some believed this to be inevitable, considering that so many had come to American shores after having gotten their fill of British oppression back home. One Hessian soldier remarked that people were free to call the eventual rebellion an American Revolution if they pleased, but the truth was that it was just a continuation of the age-old feud between the Anglicans and Presbyterians back home. That might have been an oversimplification, but there was no denying that when the Revolution broke out, a lot of Scots-Irish immediately joined the Continental Army. It is also true that a number of these new recruits were ministers.

Beyond these nascent hostilities, the French and Indian War had two other effects that made the Revolution all but inevitable—one was financial, the other was geographic.

The Seven Years' War was won by Britain at tremendous cost. Its national debt doubled during the fight, and with its local citizenry already taxed out, the British government for the first time considered direct taxes on the colonies. There already existed an economic game of cat and mouse between the Crown and the colonies that was mostly focused on trade, which meant that it was mostly focused on rum. Hands down, rum, in the years leading up to the Revolution, was New England's most important industry. Rum was the Bud Light of colonial America, where if you averaged it out, every man, woman, and child consumed four gallons a year. It is tempting to subtract out the children to make the average even more appalling, but in colonial times children and intoxicants weren't always mutually exclusive. In addition, rum was a crucial export, so valued that in some parts of the world it passed for currency. The British interest in all this primarily manifested itself in the islands it controlled in the Caribbean, which produced molasses, the primary raw material in the intoxicating beverage. The French, Dutch, and Spanish islands crushed the British islands on price, so the latter's plantation owners convinced Parliament to impose a stiff duty on sugars imported into the colonies from any non-British source. The colonies' answer to this 1733 Molasses Act was simply to smuggle cheaper molasses from other nations to its shores. The British answer to smuggling was to prosecute smugglers in colonial courts, where the smugglers had little to fear because the judges' salaries were paid by colonial legislatures, and the judges were certainly not stupid about the source of their wherewithal.

The Boston Tea Party is a celebrated event in American history, as shipments of tea were tossed into Boston Harbor and tax collectors were tarred, feathered, and forced to drink more of it than they were comfortable with. But rum was a far more important beverage, and when the British tried to control shipments of sugar and molasses for its production, businessmen had a real reason to fight. Courtesy Library of Congress.

Direct taxation on the colonies, however, was more troublesome. To pay off its debt and maintain its standing army (Britain after the French and Indian War continued to pay the salaries of a sizable army because, a century before John Maynard Keynes, it feared that throwing them all out of government work would be economically disadvantageous), Parliament began experimenting with colonial taxation on heavily used products such as paper and tea. With the exception of tea, these taxes were frequently repealed when the colonists protested.

The Boston Tea Party is among the most poorly understood events in American history—entire political movements have been launched on a fundamental misinterpretation of American history. That's somewhat forgivable, since it was not well understood, even back then. The 1773 Boston Tea Party, in which colonists tossed the modern equivalent of $1 million worth of tea into Boston Harbor, was a reaction to a decrease, not an increase, in taxes. Britain's taxes on tea and tea companies in the eighteenth century had the predictable result of raising prices and curbing demand. It also had the predictable result of making rich men of smugglers. Stunted demand led to a tea glut, and to return to equilibrium, Parliament provided the East India Company with some economic incentives that allowed it to undercut smugglers. These incentives included the right to market directly to the colonies, which is how the ships ended up in the American harbors in the first place. While good for consumers, this new, cheap tea was bad for a number of American interests including smugglers and merchants, whose interests in destroying British tea was not entirely pure.

FREDERICK lord NORTH.

British Prime Minister Lord North needed revenue to pay the costs of the French and Indian War. Since much of the war was fought in the colonies, he felt it only reasonable that the Americans pitch in to help pay for their own defense. Lacking representation in Parliament, the colonists begged to differ. Courtesy Library of Congress.

Britain's Prime Minister, Lord North, might have easily revoked the colonial tax on tea, and more than a few historians have argued he should have, to keep the peace in the colonies. He didn't, for the sake of making a statement—he wanted one and all to know that Britain had the authority to tax the colonies if it wanted to. Several dozen Boston residents, a third of whom were under the age of twenty-one, begged to differ, and the Boston Tea Party was born. Britain responded with a slate of punitive measures against Massachusetts, and any thought of a peaceful reconciliation was largely gone.

The colonists now had motive: economics. What they needed next was opportunity, and by a strange geopolitical quirk, the French and Indian War gave them that as well.

The idea that Americans might one day make a break for it was as old as America itself, and a veritable cottage industry arose in Britain out of speculating on the American future. The British were well aware of a couple of points. One, there were certainly people who sailed overseas for adventure and to seek fortune, but in the main, few people came to the New World because they were tickled with the way things were working out for them in the old. This wasn't shaping up to be a territory that longed for leadership from across the pond. Two, from the British perspective, the colonies were becoming a collection of every screwball sect and religious mutation on the face of the planet, and good luck governing that.

The more optimistic attitude was that Americans who were busy and prosperous, as they were becoming, would be happy for Britain to perform the bothersome business of governing, so long as this governing did not interfere in their growth. So this was the fine line that had to be walked: British must govern in a way the kept the colonies dependent on the mother country, without making this dependence seem in any way oppressive. Even in theory, this was asking a lot.

But in maintaining its control over the colonies, the British had two allies. Curiously enough, those allies were its enemies: the French and the Indians. Through the first three quarters of the eighteenth century, one of the colonists' primary complaints with the Crown was its failure to defend settlers from

Indian attack. Many of these attacks on the western frontier were provoked, at least in the eyes of the Indians, but settlers felt unsafe in their own homes and believed it the job of British regulars to secure the borders. To the north, the British and French had been warring over control of Lake Champlain for a hundred years, and British colonists were always wary of French encroachment from the north.

In 1759, the French were finally driven out of the Champlain Valley for good by the British, and within three years a truce had been negotiated. By this time, the British had the upper hand, having conquered the French in Canada, India, and in the sugar-producing islands of the Caribbean. The French were unlikely to cede all this territory during the peace talks, so a lively debate ensued in Britain over which lands to demand; eventually, this boiled down to a choice between Canada and Guadeloupe. The British could have one, but not both, and it was a close call.

The strategic choice was Canada. As long as the French maintained control up north, there was the risk that they might again make a push to the south, and that was one headache the British could do without—and besides, Britain already had a number of sugar islands of its own.

Guadeloupe was the economic choice. Britain's holdings in the West Indies produced enough sugar for its own use, but with Guadeloupe it would become a world power in that particular commodity. Canada was a nothing but a snow-pack overrun with furry creatures, and if the mighty British and colonial forces couldn't keep it the border safe from the French, then shame on it. Back and forth went the debate. British cabinet member William Pitt said the choice between

Canada and Guadeloupe was so contentious that it boiled down to deciding which territory he'd rather be hanged for when it was lost.

In the end, of course, the British took Canada, which—as a few eighteenth-century visionaries had predicted—had a singular unintended consequence of giving the colonists free rein to seek independence. As long as the French loomed across the border, the colonists were unlikely to split with their mother country and her considerable military presence. Once France was off the map, the balance of power was dissolved. Not only were British troops unnecessary, they were a nuisance. And nuisances needed to be expelled.

CHAPTER 2

The Hero and the Goat

At the Battle of Saratoga, Benedict Arnold—still desperately fighting for the American cause at that point—suffered a frightful injury to his left leg. Several years later, after he had thrown his lot in with the British, Arnold was conversing with a Virginia patriot about his checkered past. Arnold suggested that the grievous wound might have mitigated his punishment had he been captured by the Americans after his defection. The patriot acknowledged this might have been the case, because "we would have cut off your leg and hanged the rest."

Then, as now, there was no greater scourge in American history than Benedict Arnold.

But if Benedict Arnold's ship gone to the bottom of Lake Champlain during the Battle of Valcour Island with him in it—or if Congress had simply kept him busy fighting for freedom—he today would be remembered as an American hero, his name mentioned in the same breath as Nathaniel Greene, Daniel Morgan, and Ethan Allen. High schools and boulevards would be named after Arnold, and banners would fly in his honor.

Instead, in modern parlance, Benedict Arnold isn't so much a person as a thing—a turncoat, a traitor to his country, the lowest of the low. Going back in time to find an equally ignominious fall from grace, the great American General Greene didn't find one until he got to Satan himself. On the eve of the Civil War, eight decades after the Revolution, cartoonists looking for a way to express their disgust with southern secessionists drew them standing tooth by jowl with Benedict Arnold. In fact, Arnold's defection might make him a more familiar figure today than many patriots whose names never come up around the supper table. It's a bit hard to get an accurate read on Arnold, since no contemporary or early historian had a good thing to say about the man, any more than any modern-day terrorist benefits from sympathetic PR.

Most of Benedict Arnold (depicted in this Civil War-era cartoon with Jefferson Davis) has been condemned to the hellfires of American history, and even today he might be considered the nation's greatest villain. His left leg, however, gets a pass. Arnold performed brilliantly for the American cause at Saratoga, where he suffered a grievous foot wound. A monument at Saratoga honors Arnold's boot, although the man himself is not named. Courtesy Library of Congress.

The celebrated General Ethan Allen, by contrast, does have schools named after him. He sleeps in comfort on a lofty Wikipedia entry that assures the casual researcher that he was a "hero and a patriot," and he and his Green Mountain Boys are virtually synonymous with the ideals upon which this country was founded. He has come to represent the little guy, facing off against the barons who stack the decks of law and property to their own advantage. And he was indeed a remarkable man, deserving of fond remembrances.

But little of the Revolutionary War lends itself to neat categorization. The great events of the war—Lexington, Valley Forge, Trenton, Yorktown—mask a game of three dimensional chess that was playing out behind the scenes, as loyalties wavered and bets were hedged. To a number of colonists at the time, perhaps more than half, it would not have been entirely clear which side best represented their interests.

Arnold and Allen were two such men.

Many early stories have been told about Arnold, most all portraying him as a monster in possession of various subhuman qualities. He scattered glass on the pathway to the schoolhouse, hoping his classmates would cut their feet to shreds; he pulled young birds from their nests and tortured them to death; even his old Norwich, Connecticut, house was slandered—haunted, it was said, by Arnold's tortured soul. The wife of a subsequent owner of the home was floridly psychotic, which added to the legend, and the next family that moved in lost seven members in the space of eighteen months. Finally the poor old house was struck by lightning, shattering windows and mirrors and providing, according to one local history, an "electric shock (that) was perhaps necessary to purify it of the Arnold taint."

But there is a side of Arnold that is often ignored, for in the early days of the war there was no more innovative, scrappy, and swashbuckling patriot than Arnold himself, and he only went over to the dark side when his talents were put on the shelf by men who were either jealous of his success, or fell for trumped-up stories of Arnold's character flaws. In a somewhat petulant letter explaining his crime, Arnold in later life employed a "the leaders of the Revolution started out OK, but they went too far" defense, contending that what began as a just, defensive war had overstepped its bounds, its leaders having succumbed to the same faults they were originally fighting against.

Arnold certainly wouldn't have been the only American who felt that way, but even so, Arnold's words sound somewhat revisionist. Given everything we know about his record, it's hard to conclude that he would have become disenchanted with the battle for freedom had he been allowed to fight, instead of being placed on the sidelines where there was nothing to do but work himself into a lather against his political enemies and, by association, the colonial cause.

Arnold was doomed, writes his nineteenth-century biographer Isaac Arnold, by a system that chose its officers by political, not military, appointment. "Had Washington possessed the power of appointing and promoting officers of his army from the beginning to the conclusion of the war," he wrote, "Arnold's treason would never have been committed."

Meanwhile, Ethan Allen's own dalliances with the British are seldom mentioned in popular culture—few mention that George Washington ordered his arrest as a suspected turncoat—even though some historians view him as the bigger scoundrel of the two. Given their similarities in this regard, it was almost inevitable that they would meet on the field of battle, which they did in a most curious way.

Benedict Arnold was spoiling for a fight, almost from the day he was born. As a boy, he ran away twice to serve in colonial armies, being hauled home by his parents on the first occasion and becoming discouraged on his own on the second. He conceived a spite against the French at a young age, a point that probably came into Arnold's decision-making process in later years when France allied with the colonies—a circumstance Arnold found hard to swallow.

But as a young man, Arnold's pursuits were more commercial in nature. He was a bookseller and druggist, and maintained thirteen vessels engaged in trade (which in those days generally meant smuggling) from Canada to the West Indies, commanding his own ships on occasion. Colonial life was good to Arnold, as he set about acquiring property and raising a family. But he never seemed to shed his militant leanings. Upon learning of the Boston Massacre in 1770 he erupted, "Good god, are the Americans all asleep and tamely yielding up their liberties, or are they all turned philosophers that they do not take immediate vengeance on such miscreants?"

Allen, meanwhile, was an original American rustic, more interested in property and homespun wisdom than trade and urban finery. He was an ironworker in a Connecticut foundry, tilling the soil and hunting the rugged forests of the Green Mountains in what is now Vermont. More important, Allen commanded thousands of militiamen, the Green Mountain Boys, a band that historian Willard Sterne Randall calls "the largest paramilitary force in North America."

The enemy at the time, however, was not the British; it was New Yorkers. Allen believed his people had laid claim to Vermont (then western New Hampshire) and cemented their position by defending the lands during the French and Indian War. But New York land speculators from down south were encroaching on lands to the east of Lake Champlain, claiming that the settlers were squatters with no legal standing. New York had the lawyers, but Ethan Allen had the guns. Not surprisingly, New York authorities, when venturing into the wilds to evict the settlers, never met with anything approaching success.

So in terms of quasi-military experience, Allen and his men might have been about the most prepared when the angry words of the patriots blossomed into shots fired on a village green in the spring of 1775. The battles of Lexington and Concord were disorganized affairs, as a column of British regulars sent to seize colonial stockpiles of weapons came under attack from ever-increasing bands of American militia arriving from various locales in answer to a call to arms. It was difficult to tell who was more surprised by the American win, the British or the colonists themselves. Not everyone wanted war, and some colonists, horrified by the bloodshed, scurried back to their homes. The British soldiers took out their frustrations on the march back to Charlestown by bursting into taverns, killing a stray drunk here and there, and becoming soused themselves. At the end of the day, the British lost 250 killed and wounded, the Americans lost ninety, and the Revolutionary War was officially on.

When word of the battle reached New Haven, Benedict Arnold called townsmen to the square and whipped the public into a patriotic frenzy. There was no shortage of volunteers for action, but the town fathers were reluctant to supply the men with ammunition until Arnold—proclaiming "None but the Almighty God shall prevent my marching"—threatened to break down the doors of the magazine. The New Haven selectmen handed over the keys, and Arnold's band was off to Cambridge, Massachusetts. Once there, Arnold impressed upon the Committee of Public Safety a plan that would deliver a lightning strike at the British government, interrupt British supply lines, and seize a handsome cache of weaponry for the colonists. He would capture the poorly defended British forts on Lake Champlain at Ticonderoga and Crown Point.

As Arnold was hearing the news of Lexington and Concord in New Haven, Ethan Allen, 150 miles to the north, was receiving similar intelligence at a tavern in the town of Bennington. Allen smelled an opportunity that would assist the revolutionary cause and boost his own personal fortunes as well, and he carefully outlined his plan to his top lieutenants: He would capture the poorly defended British forts on Lake Champlain at Ticonderoga and Crown Point.

While there's some discussion over who came up with the idea first, it's likely that they came up with the same idea independently at roughly the same time. The forts were high-reward, low-risk targets that satisfied multiple objectives. Lakes Champlain and George were the interstate highways of the day, helping connect Quebec and Montreal with the Hudson River Valley and New York City. Although the lakes remained key to communications and transport, the forts at Ticonderoga, Crown Point, and St. Johns on the Canadian border had lost their sense of urgency after the French had been rousted from the Champlain Valley and the Treaty of Paris had ended the French and Indian War a decade prior.

Arnold and Allen wanted to strike a blow for the patriot cause to be sure, but dreams of personal glory weren't too far down the shopping list of reasons to take action. Both were quintessential military men, talented, strong-willed, and magnetic leaders. Along with these skills came the predictable shortcomings, as they had little use for compromise, and second opinions were as welcome as second-degree burns.

Allen had a problem with authority, and Arnold had a problem with people who had a problem with authority. Perhaps their greatest commonality, however, was that they both saw

British rule standing in the way of wealth. For Allen, ghosts of the old European feudal system were raising their ugly heads, as small landholders were always up against barons and speculators who sought to steal their land out from under them. For Arnold, British taxes and trade policies seemed to rob him of two pounds for every pound that he earned. Patriotic as they might have been in the early days of the Revolution, neither was injudicious enough to put his country's well-being ahead of his own.

But when the time came to fight, Arnold was given his start by Dr. Joseph Warren, a man Daniel Webster called "the first great martyr" of the Revolution. Warren, a revolutionary organizer who gave the go-ahead to Paul Revere's ride into history, died on Breed's Hill when he ignored his rank of Major General and fought as a private in the area of heaviest action. But when Arnold met with him in Cambridge, Warren was a leader in a Massachusetts patriotic shadow government that warmly embraced Arnold's plan and on May 3, 1775, sent him to New York with supplies and instructions to raise the necessary troops in western Massachusetts. On arriving in Stockbridge, Arnold was surprised to learn that Allen's Green Mountain boys were on the road in pursuit of the same objective. Arnold overtook the Green Mountain Boys as they were tipping back a few at a local tavern, flashed his official orders, and demanded that they recognize him as their commander.

There were no video cameras handy, so the facial reactions of Allen's backwoods ruffians to Arnold's pronouncement are sadly lost to history. He would have been quite a sight, standing before them in his military finery (in a red coat, no less), brandishing his official orders—a high-strung, legalese-spewing "banty rooster," according to one uncharitable biographer. Long story short, the Green Mountain Boys made it pretty clear that they would march under no one but Allen. With no other options, Arnold reluctantly agreed. Allen, meanwhile, lacking the formal blessing of Massachusetts (and thereby a legal basis for his actions), agreed to allow Allen and his paperwork to come along, and the two outsized commanders began an awkward, three-legged sack race to the doors of Fort Ticonderoga.

Ticonderoga, then and now, is thought of as a great military victory for the colonists, and it was certainly important on several levels. However, the handful of British who were manning the fort were not so much conquered as they were awakened in the middle of the night and informed that their services were no longer required. The news of Lexington and Concord had not yet reached the fort, so a couple of snoozing sentries had no clue why they were being roughed up by a ragtag band of marauders.

Once the raiders were in control of the fort, Arnold went straight to the magazine, Allen went straight to his writing desk, and the Green Mountain Boys went straight to the rum, an item the fort had in impressive quantities. As Arnold was inventorying the booty—much-needed cannon, rifles, ammo, and gunpowder—Allen was basically sending a personalized note to just about every important colonist in the northeast, broadcasting news of his great victory.

"Gentlemen," he wrote to the Massachusetts Congress on May 11. "I have to inform you, with pleasure unfelt before, that on the break of day of tenth of May, 1775 . . . I took the fortress of Ticonderoga by storm." His soldiers, he continued, "behaved with such restless fury, that they so terrified the king's troops that they durst not fire upon their assailants."

Allen was always better with words the second time around. He recounted in his letters that he had demanded the surrender of Ticonderoga from British Captain William Delaplace "In the name of the Great Jehovah and the Continental Congress." Other accounts had Allen simply barking, "Come out of there you goddamn old rat."

Ethan Allen's Revolutionary War cred is based almost exclusively on the British surrender of Fort Ticonderoga on Lake Champlain. The small garrison was mostly asleep and, having not yet heard about the events at Lexington and Concord, weren't clear on what Allen's band of ruffians wanted. Courtesy Library of Congress.

Expecting universal acclaim for his work, Allen was disappointed. Events were moving too fast for the more conservative members of the colonial Congresses, who still believed that reconciliation with Britain remained possible. But it was already getting a little late in the game for that. Allen's men had by now taken another British fort at Crown Point, and seized the schooner *Katherine* from the estate of Scottish officer Philip Skene, a fascinating character who had built an impressive settlement on the lake, and as recently as a month prior—as if the emerging storyline weren't complex enough—had been scheming with Ethan Allen to hoodwink the hated New York speculators by creating a new royal colony out of lands on both sides of Lake Champlain.

Unfortunately for Allen's self-narrated ride into heroic destiny, Arnold snatched the *Katherine* almost the second its captors docked it at Ticonderoga, renamed it the *Liberty*, and sailed merrily north to Canadian waters, where he seized Fort St. Johns and its naval assets, including the HMS *Royal George*, which was renamed *Enterprise*. Benedict Arnold was less at risk from the British at this point than from Ethan Allen, who was hot on his tail, furious that he didn't think of the idea first. The pair continued to threaten, snipe at, and one-up each other by pleading their cases to colonial authorities and adopting ever-escalating titles, such as "Commander of the Forts" and "Commodore of the Lake."

They might have come to real blows were it not for the Continental Congress, which instructed them to both cool their jets, retreat to the southern end of the lake, and stay put. There they were to take careful count of the weaponry they had seized from the British, on the chance that they would one day need to give it back. Among other things, this would cost the patriots an immeasurably valuable strategic position and open up all the unprotected colonials living in the upper Champlain Valley to British reprisal. Allen and Arnold duly noted Congress's concerns and lobbied instead to invade Canada.

For Ethan Allen, Ticonderoga would be the high point of the Revolution. On June 27, 1775, Congress agreed on the Quebec invasion and, bypassing Arnold, named General Philip Schuyler to lead the expedition. Allen caught up with Schuyler's force heading north to Montreal, but commanders kept the rambunctious and nettlesome Allen out of their hair by sending him on lengthy errands in the countryside. On one such sortie, Allen took it upon himself to attack Montreal, a plan that, aside from lacking manpower, strategy, and execution, made all the sense in the world. He was captured by the British, an event that might not have been universally lamented among Revolutionary leaders who shuddered at his, in Schuyler's words, "impatience and imprudence." Allen's imprisonment in America and Britain lasted nearly three years, and although he offered his services upon his release, the Continental Army politely declined to restore him to active duty.

While in captivity, Allen had been treated miserably, and there is little doubt he returned the favor with his diatribes that pushed the boundaries of lunacy. The British were almost certainly happier to release him than they had been to take him in the first place. This began a curious period in Allen's life when he and his brother—under the guise of prisoner-exchange negotiations—were at least listening to British offers of an independent province of Vermont in exchange for their loyalty. There remains to this day a contentious debate whether or not this constituted treason. Allen's defenders say he never acted on British come-hithers. But at a time when even talking to a British officer was considered to be a criminal act, his dalliances with the British certainly seem suspect. Both his political enemies and Congress charged him with treason, but by this time his star had faded to the degree that continental movers and shakers had better things to do than punch this vocal tar baby one more time. After the war, Allen continued to live in Vermont, writing *Reason: the Only Oracle of Man*, a somewhat wise-ass critique of the Bible and organized religion. (Noting Moses's account of his funeral in Deuteronomy, Allen noted that "This is the only historian in the circle of my reading, who has ever given the public a particular account of his own death.") Allen himself died in 1789 while obtaining a load of hay from what is now South Hero, Vermont.

About the time that Allen was mounting his ill-advised attack on Montreal, Arnold was set to lead an army through the wilds of Maine en route to Quebec, an epic, nearly impossible journey that for difficulty would be compared by contemporaries to Hannibal crossing the Alps. Indeed, for the next two years the colonies had no better leader than Benedict Arnold, and the American cause might have died without him.

Having been passed over for the job of leading the main offensive to Quebec—likely due to enemies made among the Green Mountain Boys during the Ticonderoga attack—Arnold got approval from Washington to march on Quebec from the southeast. Only his dogged determination prevailed in the face of innumerable miseries and misfortunes, but he made it just in time to see (although he wouldn't have known it) the British ship where Ethan Allen lay imprisoned below decks as it sailed up the St. Lawrence bound for England.

The actual siege of Quebec was a failure, and the Americans retreated to the southern end of Lake Champlain, where Arnold was able to cobble together a small naval force of seventeen newly built and captured ships that would be assigned the problematic task of matching up with the British fleet, which was superior in every way imaginable. The British sailed down the St. Lawrence to Montreal in May 1776, fortifying the Canadian city of 9,000 with troops and putting an end to any more silly ideas on the part of the colonists of invading Canada. They then moved operations to St. Johns and began assembling prefab gunboats brought from Britain. The British plan was to storm the 120-mile-long Lake Champlain, rousting colonists from the lakeside forts and providing support for a ground invasion down into the Hudson Valley that would split New England in two.

Lacking men, weapons, powder, ammunition, food, and even proper clothing, the patriots were wholly unprepared to repulse such an onslaught. They needed time to get things organized and equipped. At Crown Point, Arnold watched the calendar and the weather. A seasoned sailor himself in charge of a band of landlubbers who barely knew what part of a boat to hang the sails on, he had few delusions of victory. But in the fall of 1776, victory wasn't essential; delay would be enough. Arnold trained his ragtag band of sailors as best he could, but so poorly supplied was this little navy that it did not even have enough gunpowder for target practice.

When the winds turned to the south on October 9, the sizable British flotilla sailed out of Canada into Lake Champlain.

Two days later, about halfway down the lake, Arnold was waiting for them, his motley fleet tucked neatly out of sight behind Valcour Island on the New York side of the lake. The British didn't spot Arnold until they were downwind, and outgunned though he was, Arnold made a fight of it with the wind at his back. Though losing boats right and left, he was able to bloody the British's nose, holding them off until nightfall and then slipping through enemy lines to the Vermont side, where he put what little was left of his fleet to the torch and retreated overland to Ticonderoga.

On October 20, it snowed. Reluctantly, the British acknowledged the 1776 campaigning season was over and sailed back to Canada. Given three or four more weeks, some on the British side believed they could have mopped up then and there, snuffing out the heart of the revolt almost before it began. But the mere existence of Arnold's little navy meant the British had to advance with caution, and the tough resistance at Valcour cost them another handful of precious days.

A year later, under General John Burgoyne this time, the British were back, capturing Fort Ticonderoga in July and continuing south to Saratoga, where again Arnold lay in wait. After an inconclusive fight on September 19, the two sides closed in again on October 7. Arnold was fighting two battles, one against the British and one against his own commander, General Horatio Gates, a former British officer who was haughty in his headquarters but humble on the battlefield—effective leadership generally requiring the reverse.

Arnold, with Gates trying to call him back at almost every step, took the initiative, and the Americans won a decisive victory, one that finally convinced France to enter the war on the side of the colonists. In his report back to Congress, however, Gates took credit for the victory, and Congress obligingly minted a gold medal in his honor. Arnold, who was given no credit for the victory, called Gates "the greatest poltroon" (don't look it up, the word is superior to the definition) in the world.

His leg having been gravely wounded in the battle and with no political champions, Arnold never fought again. Washington appointed him military commander of Philadelphia after the British evacuated the city in 1778, and this inactivity contributed directly to his downfall. Arnold married eighteen-year-old Peggy Shippen, daughter of a Loyalist judge and former sweetheart of British Major John André, the man who was instrumental in convincing Arnold to switch sides. Arnold's plan to surrender West Point on the Hudson River to the British was foiled when André was captured, but although André was hanged, Arnold made his escape and lived out the rest of his life in England.

For two centuries, history, like the Continental Congress, failed to recognize Arnold's contributions to the American cause. Of late, however, his complexities have been the subject of closer investigation, just as Ethan Allen's heroism has begun to be questioned. Arnold was as prickly as he was talented, and suffered no fools. This was bound to offend a few lesser individuals at every turn, who ran complaining to the powers-that-be, either accentuating Arnold's faults or making them up wholesale. His legendary bravery—time and time again, Arnold risked his life and rallied his men from the front lines—was hard to dispute, so his enemies spread the rumor that his courage came from a bottle.

Meanwhile, the nascent government had a ridiculous formula for promoting military officers, relying on politicians, not on officers in the field, and apportioning out general-ships not by merit but by a per-colony quota. Small wonder that Arnold grew disillusioned with this new political system, which to him seemed as bad or worse than the old. When Arnold made his decision to change sides, he felt as if he were making an educated decision, one that others of his standing would want to emulate. Here, he was wrong. Four years into the war, no one on the American side was interested in fence mending. Arnold's other motivation for defection was more crass. He'd lived lavishly in Philadelphia and fallen into debt. Selling out to the British, however much it dovetailed with his philosophy, would also solve his money problems.

But the stories of Arnold and Allen somewhat typify the times. There were Loyalists and there were patriots, but there were also wide swaths of the population that would have seen lingering shades of gray. When that happened, personal interest would have come into play. Allen wanted his lands in Vermont. Arnold wanted commercial and military glory. If one side wasn't offering up the goods, why not sign up with the other? It was a war of governments, but few other wars call for individual decisions as did the American Revolution. Those individual choices created heroes and goats whose reputations have hardened over time. But in the latter half of the eighteenth century, ideas of right and wrong, good and bad, were not so easily delineated. For Benedict Arnold and Ethan Allen, their opposing places in history were little more than the luck of the draw.

Chapter 3

A Pox on the American House

In the history of hostilities the world around, few conflicts have been awarded a better name than the War of Jenkins' Ear, a conflagration waged between Britain and Spain over trade and territory in the New World. Trouble had been brewing between the antagonists for some time, when Captain Julio León Fandiño, on patrol in the West Indies in 1731 aboard the Spanish ship *La Isabela*, boarded a square-sailed brig captained by Robert Jenkins. Fandiño accused Jenkins of smuggling, which in that time period would not have been much of a reach. In the colonial age, smuggling was akin to the steroid era in baseball, where virtually everyone was doing it, but justice was spotty.

On this occasion, however, Fandiño was in no mood for games. He bound Jenkins to the mast and lopped off his ear with a cutlass, indicating he would do the same thing to the

King of England if given the opportunity. Fandiño did allow Jenkins to keep the bloody appendage, which the aggrieved captain preserved by pickling it in a jar of brine. Upon returning to England, Jenkins brandished the jar before anyone who would listen, outlining a tale of outrage that seemed to grow more colorful with each retelling. Not everyone cared. A cartoon at the time depicts an unsympathetic and marginally grossed-out Prime Minister Robert Walpole pushing away Jenkins and his ear as a fellow bureaucrat, his back to the ear-wielding Jenkins, hits on a young woman who happens to be seated nearby.

Jenkins persevered, however, and in 1739 Britain dispatched a squadron of warships to the West Indies to protect its interests. The war itself was of little consequence, but it had several notable side effects. For one, it established the military bona fides of Lawrence Washington, the older half brother of you-know-who. In fact, had anyone at the time been trolling for father-of-the-country material, many might have chosen Lawrence over George as the pony to bet on. But a strange series of events intervened, sending Lawrence to his deathbed and in the process giving George something of a shield that almost certainly helped him survive the Revolution.

During the War of Jenkins' Ear, the British for the first time called on American colonists to help fight in their wide-flung wars. Lawrence was commissioned as the senior officer in a company of Virginia infantry, and was later appointed to lead a band of marines who undertook several coastal attacks in the Caribbean. Lawrence survived the expedition, and in this he was in the minority. More than half the British forces were laid low, not by combat but by disease, and colonists who had no immunity to yellow fever and other tropical diseases were hit particularly hard.

Unfortunately, Lawrence's luck didn't hold. By 1749, his health was beginning to fail, and bouts of tuberculosis sent him from one end of the Atlantic to the other in search of a cure. Brother George was a tireless companion on these sorties, accompanying Lawrence to the mineral springs in Bath, Virginia (now Berkeley Springs, West Virginia), where as a surveyor he had learned of the healing qualities of the waters. The baths were unsuccessful, at least for Lawrence—a stone tub where George allegedly bathed with happier results remains in a state park in the heart of town—so the brothers planned a trip to Barbados, hoping that the climate might do some good. They arrived on November 2, 1751, and stayed for two months.

The warm climes didn't help clear Lawrence's lungs either. He became worse, and tried the cooler climate of Bermuda before returning to Mount Vernon, where he died in the summer of 1752.

Not only did Lawrence fail to recover while in Barbados, but his nineteen-year-old brother George became dangerously ill. Against his better judgment, George accepted a dinner invitation from a family where smallpox had recently taken up residence. Officially eradicated in 1979, smallpox had been a way of life and death on this Earth since 10,000 BC. Smallpox scars were discovered on the mummified corpse of Egyptian Pharaoh Ramses V. In the late 1700s, it was killing 400,000 Europeans annually; roughly 40 percent of those who contracted the disease failed to survive.

George Washington's initial instincts were correct. On November 17, he noted in his diary that he "was strongly attacked with the small Pox." It knocked him flat. For three weeks he was not well enough to pick up a pen. "Rare was the diarist who kept writing through the throes of smallpox," wrote Elizabeth A. Fenn in the book *Pox Americana: The Great Smallpox Epidemic of 1775–82*. "The void in Washington's diary is thus telling; its very silence speaks of a misery commonplace in years gone by but unfamiliar to the world today."

Smallpox thrived in well-traveled, generally coastal cities, but in Washington's time it was virtually unknown in rural Virginia. There were no smallpox outbreaks prior to 1747 and a scant number of Virginians would have been exposed to the disease prior to the Revolutionary War. So it was only by pure chance, and George's devotion to his brother Lawrence, that he travelled to an island that was experiencing an outbreak and became infected himself. Indeed, as it happened, it was the only foreign country that George Washington visited in his lifetime. As a teenager, George was young and strong and able to fight off the disease in a warm, favorable climate. But numerous historians have noted that had he contracted smallpox twenty-five years later in the frigid northeast in Boston or Valley Forge, he might not have been so fortunate, and the course of American history might have been quite different.

The outbreak of the Revolutionary War coincided with a debilitating outbreak of smallpox in New England, and in 1776 the real story of the war to date would not have been Lexington, Concord, Bunker Hill, or Saratoga—it would have been disease. No one knew what to do, and the reaction was predictably chaotic. It was a bizarre story that mixed religion and medicine with germ warfare and even open revolt within the ranks of the colonial army.

For the rest of the world, smallpox was an old disease with old solutions. Peoples that had experience with smallpox understood that those who contracted it once, if they survived, would be immune for life. They also understood the concept of inoculation, although their methods were a little messier than lining up for a shot from the school nurse. The Chinese, for example, would grind up and snort smallpox scabs. In India, crude smallpox inoculation had been practiced at least as far back at the year 400. These inoculations would give the patient a mild but survivable case of the pox.

In colonial America, however, inoculation was not universally known or accepted. The suffering that resulted from the disease was considered to be God's will, punishment for some past indiscretion. Short-circuiting the Almighty's criminal justice system with a little modern medicine was just asking for lightning bolts.

Although other countries had been inoculating against smallpox for centuries, Americans were slow to embrace the procedure. By the end of the eighteenth century, a safe and effective "cowpox" vaccine was available, but the process was still good grist for the nation's cartoonists. Courtesy Library of Congress.

A contrasting point of view, however, was introduced in the early eighteenth century by a Puritan minister named Cotton Mather. As monikers go, "Cotton" was somewhat an improvement over his father, whose name was "Increase"— although in the era of P-Diddy and Gaga it does not behoove us to cast stones. Cotton Mather was a complex individual, whose writings and sermons shook the firmament to its roots. It is difficult to say he was enlightened, since he went after witches like a beagle after rabbits. He did, however, think it was ridiculous that a potential answer to the smallpox problem was being ignored.

He learned of the procedure from a servant, "my Negro-man Onesimus, who is a pretty intelligent fellow," who was inoculated in Africa. Mather asked Onesimus if he had ever had smallpox and servant said, well, yes and no, explaining the inoculation process. Africans, he was told, used to "die like rotten sheep," before the practice became common of making a small incision in the arm and feeding it with pox pus. The individual, Mather wrote, became "a little sick . . . but no one ever dy'd of doing this, nor ever had the Small-Pox after it." Slave traders, in fact, inoculated Africans before shipping them overseas, in order to fetch a higher price.

The effectiveness of this process was backed up by other reports Mather had heard coming out of Constantinople, and the reverend wondered in a 1721 letter, "How does it come to pass that no more is done to bring this operation in experiment and into fashion . . . where there are thousands of people that would give many thousands of pounds to have ye Danger and Horror of this frightful Disease well over with . . ."

Of course, in the early eighteenth century, telling people you would be saving them from smallpox by infecting them with smallpox was not always an easy sell. But knowledge of the procedure, and its relative effectiveness, did exist in the colonies, even if it was not routinely put into practice. Early in the war, the British had a tremendous advantage in this arena, since they would have had more exposure to the disease, and therefore immunity. Those recruits to the army who were not immune were inoculated as a matter of policy. In fact, they used this immunity to their advantage by trying to spread smallpox among their enemies by sending infected people and clothing into enemy camps. The evidence is sketchy and circumstantial, but there seems to be enough smoke to imply fire.

Biological and chemical warfare, of course, were not new. Black Death–infected corpses had been catapulted into walled cities during the Middle Ages, and in South America, fires fueled by hot chili peppers were built upwind of the enemy, sending a blinding wall of smoke into the fray. So the British would not have been unfamiliar with similar tricks. Following the unsatisfactory (for the Indians) conclusion of the French and Indian War in 1763, Native Americans rose up one more time when they discerned that the British were more difficult to deal with than the French. Dating back to the days of Samuel de Champlain, the French had interacted with the Native Americans through negotiations and alliances; the British preferred the iron fist. The brief Indian rebellion was given the name of Pontiac's War, after an Ottawa chief instrumental in raiding lightly defended British forts. The uprising blindsided British conquering General Jeffrey Amherst, who had little regard for the Indians in any respect, including their abilities in warfare. The 500 soldiers and colonists who, in fear for their lives, squeezed into Fort Pitt at present-day Pittsburgh would have begged to differ. For almost two months under Indian siege, they suffered from all manner of discomforts, including an outbreak of smallpox.

Amherst was not above using this minor outbreak to his advantage. In a letter to Colonel Henry Bouquet in the summer of 1763, Amherst wrote, "You will Do well to try to Innoculate the Indians by means of Blankets, as well as to try Every other method that can serve to Extirpate this Execrable Race. I should be very glad your Scheme for Hunting them Down by Dogs could take Effect, but England is at too great a Distance to think of that at present." Bouquet, who was preparing to lead a force to relieve Fort Pitt, wrote back affirming that he would indeed try to circulate some infected blankets among the Indians once he got there.

Back at the fort, however, the increasingly desperate colonists and soldiers were way ahead of Amherst and Bouquet. According to at least one account, two Delaware Indians approached the fort under a flag of truce, demanding its surrender. The British officers refused, but to show their hearts were in the right place they presented the pair with "gifts" that included smallpox-infected blankets and a handkerchief. The results of this subterfuge are not clear. Smallpox did break out among the Delaware, but there's no conclusive evidence the Fort Pitt blankets had anything to do with it. The two Indians who approached the fort were seen again and never seemed the worse for wear. And the timing of the would-be exposure and the eventual outbreaks did not appear to match based on eyewitness accounts.

Nevertheless, the British had a track record in these matters on April 19, 1775, when, after being rudely treated at Lexington and Concord, they were forced back within the confines of the city of Boston. Their position was tenuous at best, as the rebels populated the high ground around Boston harbor. The patriot militia laid siege to the city as best they could with limited weaponry and organization. The effect was somewhat limited in that the patriots had no way to deny access to the sea to cut off supply ships and reinforcements. But it was still an uncomfortable position for British soldiers and Loyalists, what with rebel guns bristling from the hilltops. On June 17, the British tested the Americans' resolve by attacking a peninsula across a channel to the north of Boston in what became known as the Battle of Bunker Hill. The British won the battle, but at a cost so high—more than 1,100 men killed or wounded—that they refrained from any more direct attacks.

By summer of 1775, the siege still intact, Congress had minted the Continental Army, with George Washington as its commander in chief. Washington arrived in Boston on July 2 and immediately saw to two important tasks—fortifying the entrenchments and establishing a quarantine camp for those with smallpox. It was the latter effort that likely had the greater effect. Through the second half of 1775, the two sides engaged in a limited brand of hostilities, mainly consisting of raids, skirmishes, and sniper fire. With the approaching winter, the British were growing more anxious with their situation, and began to at least consider a biological means of attack. This they allegedly accomplished by sending people infected with smallpox across enemy lines into continental camps.

Again, no direct evidence exists. Washington initially dismissed reports that smallpox-infected refugees were being sent into colonial camps. The British might resort to such skulduggery where mere savages were concerned, but it would never unleash a deadly epidemic against what were still effectively its own people, he thought. Yet as time went on, and more evidence accumulated, Washington decided he would have to take the reports seriously.

Even if only psychologically, the disease gave the British a meaningful advantage due to their own immunity. The continentals, some of whom had arrived from outlying colonies where smallpox was virtually unknown, were understandably terrified of every last lesion or pimple. Moreover, despite successes with inoculations elsewhere, there was still a religious and also a patriotic resistance to what would have passed for modern medicine at the time. (They might have been justly proud of their descendants who, two centuries down the road, would feel much the same way about fluoride.) Forced inoculations amounted to a loss of freedom, and colonists weren't running around putting up liberty poles for nothing. Even after the relatively safe cowpox (a mild relative of smallpox) vaccine was developed at the end of the eighteenth century, cartoonist James Gilroy lampooned the process with an etching of panicked calves bursting out of the arms of those who had been inoculated.

Even prior to the Revolutionary War, smallpox vaccinations had been a national topic of discussion and even legislation. Virginia outlawed vaccinations in 1769 after riots against the practice broke out in Norfolk County. The procedure was distrusted among Americans on multiple fronts.

The inoculations were usually safe, key word "usually." Out of every 100 individuals who were inoculated, one or two would die, which was at least cause for concern, if not alarm. Along with the philosophical concerns, there were logistical problems as well. Once infected with the vaccine, a person could easily spread the disease among friends and neighbors unless a strict quarantine was maintained. These logistical problems exponentially increased when trying to fight a war.

Washington himself supported inoculations, but vaccinating an army wasn't a simple thing. He felt the army could not be vaccinated at once, for fear that the British might find out—spies on both sides were in abundance—and attack while the men were debilitated. But inoculating piecemeal was risky as well. Should infected soldiers accidentally come in contact with those who had not been inoculated, the remainder of the army was at risk.

As both Washington and Congress were failing to make up their minds, a number of soldiers took matters into their own hands, in direct violation of orders. The inoculation process required no medical genius—a shallow incision into the arm or a pinprick under a fingernail dressed with a little pus from a smallpox sore, and that was basically all there was to it. In the early years, much extraneous, preparatory voodoo—perhaps to give patients the idea that they were getting their money's worth—accompanied the process, but gradually, unnecessary complexity went by the boards. The patient could expect to be sick for about three weeks, but even a mild case of smallpox wasn't terribly pleasant—it spoke to how terrified the troops were of catching the disease "in the normal way," as they put it, that they would subject themselves to the risk and discomfort. Further, self-inoculation was strictly prohibited in the army and could result in severe punishment for men or doctors who were caught in the act. But even these threats had little effect. Men who had once wanted freedom from inoculation now wanted the freedom to inoculate.

Washington's quick action to limit interaction and establish separate smallpox hospitals largely saved the Boston troops, but those with designs on capturing the cities of Montreal and Quebec weren't as fortunate. The campaign north after the capture of the Lake Champlain forts in the spring of 1775 should have been a piece of cake. The cities were lightly defended and French Canadians (having been conquered by the British themselves sixteen years earlier) were disposed to look upon the Americans as liberators. But the campaign began too late in the year, ran into multiple delays, and ended in disaster for the Americans at Quebec in the middle of a blizzard on the last day of 1775. And while the redcoats and their Indian allies certainly had a hand in the American defeat, the real culprit was smallpox. Conditions in the American camps were brutal, and those who contracted smallpox suffered miserably from cold and hunger, along with wretched back and head pain, fever, and dripping sores erupting on their skin and even inside their mouths and nasal passages. Soldiers ignored orders against inoculation and frantically sought vaccinations, often with the support and facilitation of their immediate officers, who did not have the luxury afforded Congress to mull the problem at its leisure.

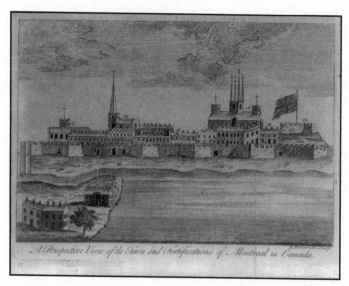

A Perspective View of the Town and Fortifications of Montreal in Canada.

Early in the war, Montreal and Quebec were lightly defended and should have been ripe for the colonial picking. But more than the British, smallpox prevented Americans from capturing Canada. Courtesy Library of Congress.

The British reinforced Quebec in the spring of 1776, but by then it hardly mattered. Nearly half of the 1,900 members of the Continental Army were sick, and there was nothing to do but retreat southward. Fresh troops reached the Continentals at the border, but without effective quarantines, these troops were quickly infected as well. "Smallpox is ten times more terrible than Britons, Canadians and Indians together," wrote John Adams to his wife Abigail. "This was the cause of our precipitate retreat from Canada." By the time the epidemic had run its course, more than 1,000 soldiers had died of the disease, far more than had been killed in battle. (This was true of the war as a whole, where of the conservatively estimated 25,000 American dead, only 8,000 died from their wounds.)

In Boston, things were working out better, at least temporarily. The British succumbed to the American siege and evacuated the city on March 17, 1776. This was both good and bad. When the two parties were engaged in their eleven-month stare-down, people on both sides of the lines stayed put. When the British left, there was a pent-up demand for travel, which introduced the virus to a whole new set of unsuspecting victims. This renewed outbreak convinced Massachusetts to lift its prohibition on vaccines, leading Boston to engage in one of the more innovative social-behavior experiments of the war. Typically, those who were inoculated were sequestered at home or hospital to prevent them from contaminating others. Boston took the opposite approach. Town fathers encouraged residents to seek vaccinations and then move about the city all they pleased. The onus would be on smallpox deniers to either get out of town or stay put in their homes. It worked. Thousands of people from the town and surrounding countryside swarmed the city to be treated. "For ten days the entire city of Boston would be turned into a giant smallpox hospital," wrote University of South Carolina professor Woody Holton.

By 1776, many familiar figures—Thomas Jefferson, Martha Washington, John and Abigail Adams—and other people of means had already been inoculated. The poor were not as fortunate, and, to add insult to injury, were sometimes exposed to smallpox by the careless behavior of those whose inoculations had made them contagious. Containment was out of the question, particularly in cities such as Philadelphia, where there was heavy traffic and the contagious mingled tooth by jowl with the non-immune. Into this mix came military recruits who had no protection from the disease whatsoever.

In early 1777, the time had come. Washington, with the approval of Congress, ordered medical personnel to vaccinate the men, a process that had to be done in utmost secrecy lest the British find out and use the army's weakened state to its advantage. In the end, however, fear of the disease was stronger than fear of the enemy.

In more ways than one, smallpox had left its mark. It discouraged men who had not been exposed from volunteering for service. Fenn quotes Washington's younger brother John Augustine, who told the general, "I know the dainger of the small pox and camp fever is more alarming to many than any daniger they apprehend from the arms of the enemy." Officers and their men always lived in fear of another outbreak, and secret inoculations eroded military discipline. Whether the British were engaged in germ warfare or not, they were in the colonials' heads. At the very least, the immune British soldiers could use infected civilians as human shields, preventing the Continental Army from risking a battle that would take them in close proximity to the sick. And of course, in the middle of a war, the logistics were a nightmare. The sick had to be treated, quarantines had to be maintained, and the routine flow of army activity was impeded at every turn. In the end, Washington had no choice. The war would be hard enough to win on even terms. With the vulture of smallpox on the army's shoulders for the duration of the war, the fledgling Continental Army would have stood little chance.

Chapter 4
Floating Extermination Camps

Ebenezer Fox did not start out to be a sailor. He did not start out to be much of anything. At age seven he was deemed strong enough to be of some commercial use, so his father hired him out to a nearby farmer, and the boy grew up in what he took to be unfair circumstances. He might not have felt that way, except that he was born in 1763 and all through his formative years he heard talk of freedom and liberty, rights and representation. As he gazed around the barnyard, none of these ideals seemed to apply to him.

So, decades in advance of Huck Finn, he ran away for an adventure that would make a raft on the Mississippi look like a game of Parcheesi.

Life events for the young Fox lined up with almost cosmic perfection. He was born in the year that saw the end of the French and Indian War, a conflict that was tougher on the frontier colonists than on the soldiers who fought it. The colonies sent militia to aid the British regulars, and for their trouble were rewarded in subsequent years with taxes on their most popular goods, trade restrictions, and no voice in Parliament to speak in opposition to it all.

In 1770, when Fox was paternally volunteered for a life of toil, a verbal exchange between a British private and a wig-maker's apprentice escalated into a showdown between a mob of angry Bostonians and a handful of British soldiers. A shot rang out, striking and killing a runaway slave named Crispus Attucks, who is widely considered to be the first casualty of the American Revolution. Four more Americans would die, and a point of no return was likely passed in an event that became popularly known as the Boston Massacre.

Both the colonies and young Fox felt put upon. "A spirit of disaffection pervaded the land," he wrote in an eventful memoir. "Groans and complaints, and injustice and wrongs were heard on all sides . . . almost all the conversation that came to my ears related to the injustice of England and the tyranny of government."

This imprint of discontent soon stamped itself on many youngsters who were serving their parents against their will. The young colonial boys looked at the oppression suffered by their folks and then at their own oppression and calculated that, on the whole, they had it harder than their fathers. The doctrine of taxation without representation, if you thought about it long enough, could apply to slopping hogs and split-ting rails without being afforded the opportunity to vote on it: "I thought I was doing myself a great injustice to remain in bondage, when I ought to go free; and that the time was come, when I should liberate myself from the thralldom of others, and set up government of my own; or, in other words, do what was right in the sight of my own eyes."

Along with a friend named John Kelley who felt as oppressed as he did, the twelve-year-old Fox quit Boston and set out for the Rhode Island seacoast on April 18, 1775—the day before the British marched on Lexington and Concord. The boys were ignorant of this great historic event, which led to no small amount of confusion on their trip south. As they trudged into each new town along the way, great crowds starved for news from Boston would turn out en masse when they saw travelers approaching from the north. In a serious misinterpretation of the facts on the ground, the youth assumed that all the towns-folk on their route south had been alerted by the authorities to be on the lookout for two wayward boys who had ditched their responsibilities and flouted the wishes of their parents.

The boys reached the wharf in Providence and in the name of efficiency agreed to split up to look for work. They neglected, however, to settle on a time and place for a rendezvous, and Fox never saw John Kelley again. He did, however, land employment as a cabin boy on a ship bound for the Caribbean seeking a load of coffee and molasses. After two weeks, the ship dropped anchor in the Cape Francois harbor on the island of modern-day Haiti. Being a French island at the time, trade with the colonies was illegal. This obstacle was overcome with a few winks and carefully selected merchants who thought British trade restrictions were as pointless as the Americans did. Smuggling was not terribly difficult at the time because of a quirk written into colonial law—while governors, judges, and custom agents were legally answerable to the

Crown, they were paid by the local legislatures. So the letter of the law ran smack into the reality that it was financially prudent for the judicial system to overlook naughty sea captains.

Two weeks after the crew had assembled the necessary barrels and loaded its illicit cargo, it returned to Stonington, Connecticut, to learn that in its absence the Revolutionary War had commenced. The men were to get a quick taste of the hostilities; on the final leg to Providence, their ship was overtaken by the British. The American sailors were given permission to swim for the coast, which the young Fox reached ". . . Nearly exhausted from fatigue and fear, not a little augmented by the sound of the bullets that whistled around my head while in the water." Invigorated by the adventure, the boy immediately signed up for another tour of the Caribbean.

Fox was eventually persuaded at age sixteen to pursue a more traditional career, and he apprenticed with a Boston barber and wigmaker named John Bosson. The barber was one of those who preferred to live life beneath the churning surface of current events without actively taking part. Thus, when his name came up in a draft of Massachusetts militia for a march on New York, Bosson became almost physically ill. Fox wrote dryly that "Although a firm friend to his country, and willing to do all he could to help along her cause, as far as expressing favorable opinions and good wishes . . . there was an essential difference in his mind between the theory and the art of war . . . The idea of shouldering a musket, buckling on a knapsack, leaving his quiet family, and marching several hundred miles for the good of his country, never took a place in his mind." In this, Bosson was by no means alone in colonial America at the time.

Fox volunteered to go in his stead, his master being good enough to see to the details of the boy's enrollment in a regiment before he had a chance to change his mind. The march had little consequence, as by the time of their arrival General Washington had abandoned his idea of attacking New York, and the regiment disbanded. Fox returned to his vocation and swore off military life for good, a vow that lasted for about a year, when he again got the itch and signed on with the new twenty-one-gun Massachusetts ship *Protector*, whose job was to interfere with the all-too-effective British blockade. As a willing sailor, Fox was in the minority. Most had to be coerced with appeals to manhood, promises of riches (these promises were largely false, except that crew members were awarded a share of the booty for each captured enemy ship) and, most effectively, a surplus of rum. Fox related that the resulting scene was memorable: "Upwards of three hundred and thirty men were carried, dragged, and driven on board, of all kinds, ages and descriptions, in all the various stages of intoxication; from that of 'sober tipsiness' to beastly drunkenness, with the uproar and clamor that may be more easily imagined than described. Such a motley group has never been seen since Falstaff's ragged regiment paraded the streets of Coventry." Once everyone was on board, the gangplank was pulled and the *Protector* drifted into the harbor before anyone had a chance to sober up.

In the summer of 1780, *Protector* gained its sea legs in a successful battle against a sizable thirty-two-gun privateer, the *Admiral Duff*. Privateers were heavily armed merchant ships carrying letters of marque, or special permission from the home country, to attack and plunder enemy boats. Under the letters of marque, private shipping companies could make some money on the side, and the monarchy was able to indirectly fight naval battles without having to buy new boats. It was an effective but bizarre arrangement that would be a little like if the US government allowed Federal Express drivers to arm their trucks and go after Purolator.

Admiral Duff's size worked against it. Its guns overshot the smaller *Protector*, and did considerable damage to the sails and rigging, but little to the superstructure and crew. By contrast, the *Admiral Duff* was splintered and set afire by enemy shot. When flames reached the ship's powder magazine, the resulting fireball sprayed the sea with burning timber, canvas, and men. *Protector*'s crew pulled fifty-five British sailors out of the water and treated their wounds as best they could. *Protector* followed up on its success by cruising the Caribbean and picking off several British ships, which stood to profit Fox and the rest of the crew quite handsomely on their return to Boston. They never made it.

A few days out of Boston, *Protector* was chased down and captured by two ships of superior strength. An American sailor who was captured by the British during the Revolution would notice two key differences from those captured in accordance with the Geneva Convention, neither of them good. Most significant was that the British considered the war to be a rebellion, and therefore considered those who were captured to be traitors instead of prisoners of war. The distinction mattered, because the British—as Fox was about to find out—felt no obligation to treat their captives with any degree of respect or humanity. Nor did the established practices between warring nations regarding parole and prisoner exchange apply; since the British didn't recognize the American Congress, there was theoretically no opposing government with which to negotiate. From a legal standpoint, this presented other problems. If the rebels were indeed British subjects, they would be afforded certain legal rights that—seeing as how British courts were ill-equipped to process thousands of traitors at a time—were somewhat impractical. On March 3, 1777, Parliament temporarily suspended habeas corpus for those who were charged with treason in the colonies or on the high seas.

Here, the judicial process began to differentiate between soldiers on land and sailors and privateers at sea, and not in a way that would be favorable to Fox. Although Britain sanctioned privateers itself, it viewed privateers from other nations as lower than low and basically no different from pirates. So while there was some effort, with eventual success, to work out a parole and POW exchange with Congress on land, there was no such urgency on behalf of Fox and his fellow sailors, who were committed to prison ships and forgotten.

But imprisonment was not necessarily the worst thing that could happen. The British felt quite within their rights to compel the biggest and strongest men to fight on the side of the King wherever and whenever battle was required. Fox explained, "In this manner was many an American citizen, in the morning of life, dragged from his country, his friends, and his home; forced on board of a ship of war; compelled to fight against his own country; and, if he lived, to fight in battle with other nations, against whom he had no feelings of hostility. Many a one spent his whole life in foreign service, far from his native land, while his relatives were ignorant of his fate, till, worn out with toil and wounds, a shadow of his former self, he dropped into the grave unpitied and unknown."

Short and slight, Fox was spared this indignity. But it was small comfort, since instead he was sent into the heart of one of the darkest corners of the Revolutionary War—the prison ship they called *Jersey*, or, as it was more commonly known, "Hell Afloat."

The British controlled little territory in colonial America that they could be confident of holding. Therefore, they had few reliable places on which to build prison camps. The solution was to anchor hulks of worn-out ships, sixteen in all, offshore and jam them as many prisoners as their groaning timbers would hold.

The HMS *Jersey* began life in 1736 as a sixty-gun ship of the line, which essentially meant that it was designed to be one floating link in a chain of ships that would face off against a similarly configured line of enemy ships and blast away until one side or the other blinked. In the nautical arms race, the *Jersey* was soon left behind. In 1765, the 100-gun HMS *Victory*— Lord Nelson's flagship at the 1805 Battle of Trafalgar—set the standard, a ship so massive it required 100 acres of oak forest to construct. The *Jersey* did yeoman duty for the British Navy for thirty-five years until March of 1771, when she was hauled up into the mudflats of Wallabout Bay, west of the present-day borough of Brooklyn. Her masts and spars were sawn down and she was fashioned into a hospital ship where, had it not been for the Revolution, her existence would have been lost to history. Instead, she became the most notorious of the hulks the British used to confine American prisoners.

The prison ships were probably Britain's darkest legacy of the Revolution. They did not reflect poor judgment in the heat of the battle or an emotional reaction to some provocation or another. By all appearances, they represented a slow mass execution of men the British regarded as traitors without having to spend money on rope. The colonials were aware of the atrocity, but powerless to do anything about it. Washington strongly appealed to the British sense of decency, to no avail.

More men died on the prison ships than in battle. The commonly cited number of deaths is 11,500, but some estimates are as high as 18,000. Those who were cast into the bowels of the prison ships and lived to write about it later all recalled the horror of their first impressions. The prisoners they saw resembled some subhuman or ghoul-like species, sallow skin stretched over a collection of lurching bones, some catatonic, some raving, blubbering, praying, or crying for home. Disease had driven some of them mad. Malnutrition, gastronomic systems treated to decaying rations, disease, and a lack of sanitation created conditions belowdecks so fetid and rank that lamps lacked the oxygen it took to burn. *Jersey's* reputation had proceeded her, Fox wrote: "The idea of being incarcerated in this floating Pandemonium filled us with horror; but the idea we had formed of its horrors fell far short of the realities . . . I now found myself in a loathsome prison, among a collection of the most wretched and disgusting looking objects that I had ever beheld in human form."

He was not alone in his assessment. "Our situation . . . was uncomfortable almost beyond endurance. We were so crowded that we could not either sit or lie down," wrote Christopher Hawkens, who as a lad had been pressed into duty as a cabin boy for a British naval officer, escaped, and three years later signed up with a privateer because life as a farm hand had not been stirring enough for him. He'd been back at sea less than a week when his ship was captured by two British frigates and the crew sent to the sullen hulk of the *Jersey*.

The first night was spent bellowing out patriotic songs, much to the consternation of their captors. The frivolity lasted a day before reality sank in. Hawkins jammed himself into a crevice of the ship, which unfortunately was on the main path to the hatch above-decks, where terribly ill men went during the night to either throw up or suffer through bouts of diarrhea. Only two were allowed topside at once, which meant that individuals standing in line often couldn't wait before an eruption of one sort or another. "This induced an almost constant running over me by the sick, who would besmear myself and others with their bloodying loathsome filth," Hawkens wrote. Men who had extensive stays on the *Jersey* understandably became as animals, and the guards made sport of turning them against each other. Prisoners took their rations in gangs of six, and when one man was caught stealing more than his share, he was stripped and the other five were encouraged to strike him with the six-foot paddle that the cook used to stir the gruel. By the time the second took his turn, the poor wretch was bleeding and on the verge of unconsciousness. Hawkins continued, "A second man took the instrument and with no less mercy than the first inflicted six more strokes—the blood and flesh flying ten feet at ev'ry stroke." The man fainted and was resuscitated long enough to receive more blows before fainting again. Again he was revived and his wounds doused with beef brine. It no longer mattered. In two days the man was dead.

The vermin, it almost goes without saying, were the prime beneficiaries of the conditions. At one point Hawkins watched in horror as a man stripped off his shirt, collected a generous handful of lice, and calmly stuffed them in his mouth. It was hardly any better or worse than the average daily fare. Hard, moldy biscuits had to be pounded on the deck to divest them of their worms. The pork bore a suspicious resemblance to some undistinguished sea creature and the only time the salt beef was tender enough to cut when it had decayed to the point of flaccidity. Even less appetizing was the manner of preparation, which invariably involved boiling you-name-it in water hauled up from the shallows—the same water into which the wastes of a thousand men were routinely tossed. The salt water would corrode the copper kettles, facilitating a chemical change that stoked physical and mental illnesses.

Prisoner accounts estimate that six to ten men would succumb to these conditions each day. It was difficult to tell, because belowdecks a corpse could lie around for a week before it distinguished itself from the general population. Each day, the bodies were stacked on the forecastle and then lowered into a small boat for transport to the shore. There they were buried in shallow graves in soft ground that was constantly being eroded by the East River. This became an issue when the shoreline was eaten away at the site of the mass graves, and bones and skulls began unceremoniously popping out of the bank. The remains were eventually gathered and reinterred in 1808. As development took over the general area, the bones bounced around to a couple of locations before finding their final resting place in Brooklyn's Fort Greene Park in 1873 under a hundred-foot granite column designed by Stanford White. (An earlier memorial had been designed by Central Park designer Frederick Law Olmsted, meaning that if nothing else these poor souls garnered the attention of two of the nation's most celebrated architects.)

Outside of death, there were two other ways off the ship—one was escape, the other was to enlist in the Royal Navy. Christopher Hawkins chose the former, Ebenezer Fox the latter.

Escape attempts from the *Jersey* were common, but successful escapes weren't. Sentries lined the shore, so swimming parallel to the land for a couple of miles was necessary to escape their jurisdiction. New York remained a Loyalist stronghold, so even if an escapee made landfall, there were few assurances of finding a sympathetic comrade who could provide food or transportation. While most escape attempts ended in death, the ones that succeeded were almost poetic. Perhaps the most storied occurred when, according to Fox, "a boat came alongside (the *Jersey*) containing a number of gentlemen from New York, who came for the purpose of gratifying themselves with the sight of the miserable tenants of the prison ship; influenced by the same kind of curiosity that induces some people to travel a great distance to witness an execution." The British on board the *Jersey* paid these dandies such consideration that they forgot to keep an eye on a handful of prisoners, who in a blink lowered themselves into the yawl and made their getaway. For good measure, one of the escapees responded to futile British musket shots by mooning his former captors.

Hawkins and a cohort chose a route straight out of the *Shawshank Redemption* playbook, breaking through stout iron bars on a belowdeck portal during a thunderstorm, coinciding the blows of their crowbars with thunderclaps. The two lowered themselves into the water and, thanks to a miscommunication, never saw each other again. Hawkins swam for two hours in the chilly October water before it became apparent he could go no further while towing a heavy knapsack filled with his clothing and bottle of rum. He cut the appendage loose just minutes before the water became shallow enough to wade. Naked and hungry, he journeyed the length of Long Island to Sag Harbor, where he had friends sympathetic to the patriots' cause. Along the way he talked his way into a suit of clothes and enough food to get by; he was captured by some Loyalist rabble in Oyster Bay and condemned to the gallows, but managed to get away before the unfortunate event could take place. Hawkins reported a number of similarly close shaves and could have been killed any number of times by Loyalists, who were convinced that the "damned rebels" were fighting a lost cause and didn't mind telling him so. Undoubtedly, this made it all the more sweet when, the day after his safe arrival in Sag Harbor, he learned that Cornwallis had surrendered at Yorktown.

Fox's route, by contrast, was longer and infinitely more complex. Given the prospects of staying on the *Jersey* for an open-ended term or serving in the Royal Navy, he finally chose the latter, a decision that caused him more than a little anguish. He was promised he would not be called on to fight against his home country, and would instead do garrison duty in Jamaica. As might be expected, this was a far more comfortable life than rotting away in the *Jersey*. Even better, the British commander learned that Fox was an expert wigmaker who would be much use in spiffing the officer up for formal balls. In this role, Fox earned considerable trust—too much, as it would turn out. He was allowed to roam the town of Kingston whenever he pleased, and used the relative freedom to hatch an escape plan, which he successfully executed with four other Americans who had been pressed into service.

Fox's band of men crossed the length of Jamaica in a trip fraught with peril that much resembled Hawkins's skedaddle across Long Island. From the north coast, the crew commandeered a small boat, sailed to Cuba, and eventually connected with an American frigate headed for France. It was in Bordeaux, awaiting new orders, that they learned of the war's end in 1783. The news, curiously enough, was not well received: "(T)his news, so highly prized in the United States, produced much misery and distress among the seamen in foreign ports." The sailors were immediately discharged from service, which meant—unless they were independently wealthy, which they weren't—they had no way book passage home. Fox was fortunate enough to find a Boston-bound French brig in need of hands. When it weighed anchor, "We . . . set sail for our native land—a land of freedom, where I anticipated, with emotions that cannot be described, the pleasure of meeting with relations and friends, from whom I had so long been absent, and where I hoped to enjoy the sweets of liberty, without anything to molest or make me afraid." He returned home after a three-year absence into the arms of his weeping mother, who had long since given him up for dead.

The *Jersey* simultaneously released its gruesome cargo, ending its military career and closing a final, unspeakable chapter in the Revolution. But still, she wouldn't go away. For years she sat sullen and abandoned, no one wanting to get close for fear of exposure to the contagions within. Finally, in a fitting end, it burned to the waterline.

Chapter 5
Starting a Navy from Scratch

Today, Lake Champlain is a well-kept vacation secret, a long, narrow jewel nestled between the Green Mountains of Vermont and New York's Adirondacks. Except to those privy to its charms, it contentedly passes the years out of sight and mind of the American psyche. But in colonial times, the lake was the center of the universe. It was perfectly balanced among Montreal and Quebec to the north, New York and Philadelphia to the south, and Boston to the east. Combining with the Richelieu and St. Lawrence rivers in Canada and Lake George and the Hudson to the south, it was a colonial superhighway in the days when traveling overland in the colonial interior was an achingly slow process.

The lake is the only natural feature that the great explorer Samuel de Champlain saw fit to name after himself. It was on the southern end of the lake on the New York side that he introduced the Mohawk Indians to the effectiveness of the European shotgun, killing two chiefs with one blast and altering the northeastern Native American balance of power in one puff of acrid smoke. Better than a century and a half after this confrontation, the British, formerly French, Fort Ticonderoga occupied the site of Champlain's brief battle, and this remote ink spot in the colonial wilderness was about to witness the a second cataclysmic event in the course of North American history.

Six weeks after Patrick Henry issued his liberty or death ultimatum, and three weeks after Lexington and Concord, colonial militia surprised the fifty British soldiers garrisoned at Ticonderoga, taking control of one of the colonies' most strategic locations and seizing dozens of cannon and sundry military equipment in the process. The following winter, Henry Knox, a chubby bookworm who was about to become the Continental Army's Chief Artillery Officer, led an epic expedition through snowy mountains and icy rivers to haul fifty-nine big guns, averaging about a ton apiece, to the outskirts of Boston. Once in place in the heights surrounding Boston, they were instrumental in driving the British out of the city.

Where guns, ships, and equipment were concerned, the Continental Army frequently had to improvise. Congress originally thought it might have to give the guns captured at Fort Ticonderoga back to the British, but when hostilities escalated, the cannon were sent overland to Boston, an impossibly tricky task overseen by the owner of a Boston book store. Courtesy National Archives.

But just as significantly, the patriots—now having a toehold on the lake—were in critical need of boats. They were not alone. As colonists from Maine to Georgia came to the realization they had a war on their hands in the spring of 1775, they also quickly understood that they would need some semblance of a navy. It was a long step, however, from rousing speeches around the liberty pole to comprehensive construction of warships.

The story of the colonial navy is not one of overpowering success. In fact, it led to some of the most abject disasters of the war. But even so, it contributed some tales of amazing ingenuity and groomed a class of naval commanders that would be ready when the British came calling again in 1812. In the end, the odd patchwork of makeshift warships—some converted merchant ships, some hastily cobbled out of green wood, some little more than an oversized rowboat with a miniature cannon in the prow—were able to do just enough. This floating curio cabinet seldom won against its far superior opponent, but it harassed, delayed, and diverted the great British Navy at crucial times during the war.

Nowhere was there a better example of this than on Lake Champlain in the autumn of 1776, where the British on the north end of the lake and the colonists on the south had spent the summer in a hasty round of shipbuilding. While the British were largely assembling prefabricated parts brought from home, the colonists had their hands full trying to encourage coastal shipwrights to pick up and venture into the howling wilderness, where local carpenters were more experienced in building oxcarts. When the two sides were ready for battle, the British had twenty-five warships and fifty boats for support to the colonists' fifteen, and two of the British ships alone had more guns than the Americans' entire fleet.

It was the plan of General Guy Carleton to send his ships with 700 sailors south to annihilate the American navy, while another 1,700 foot soldiers and Indians shadowed the British fleet in transports and on the New York shore. The army would continue south to New York City, controlling the Champlain and Hudson valleys and splitting the colonies right through the heart. It would be a quick end to the rebellion, and all that stood between the British and success were a handful of ships under future traitor Benedict Arnold, manned by five hundred newly minted sailors who knew nothing of ships.

But Arnold chose his position brilliantly, and although he would lose every ship he had, he was able to delay the British advance for a very meaningful ten days. On October 20 it began to snow, and Carleton realized it was too late in the season to maintain his rebellion-ending campaign. The British forces were aware they had come oh, so close, but that American ships had done just enough to throw them off their game. Perhaps most emblematic of the British campaign was a time-consuming battle fought with a stubborn foe that refused to give in.

On the night of the battle that had left the American fleet in splinters, Carleton's ships pinned the remaining American vessels behind Valcour Island on the New York side of the lake. It was widely assumed the British would mop up the next day. But a dark night and a heavy fog enabled Arnold to slip through the lines, much to the disbelief of the British command. Despite the fog, the British immediately began to search for the missing ships, which they felt certain must be nearby. Sure enough, a hulking shadow slipped into view, and the British gunboats opened up with all they had. Initially they were encouraged when they experienced no fire in return, assuming the targeted boat was out of ammunition.

British cannon fire smoke mixed with the fog complicated identifying the ship, which was proving incredibly resilient. As the assault went on into the morning, the target refused to go down. It wasn't until a breeze cleared the smoke and fog that the British commanders realized they'd spent the past hour shooting at a small island that was entirely unimpressed with British firepower. Today the little island is known alternately as Gunboat Rock or Carleton's Prize, the rust stains from deteriorating cannonballs visible as a reminder of the campaign's ultimate futility.

The British, of course, were the technical victors of this particular confrontation, islands notwithstanding. Among American ships that were destroyed by Carleton or burned by the colonists to keep them out of enemy hands, the British went 15 for 15. The tiny Champlain Navy was gone, as Arnold and his men ditched their remaining ships, put them to the torch, and fled south to Crown Point. The British would again try to split the colonies in two the following year, an effort that looked good until Saratoga on the Hudson River, where the Americans finally proved their mettle sufficiently to lure France into the war.

But in the early years of the war, the colonists would have to depend on makeshift navies such as the one on Lake Champlain to nip at British nautical heels. So superior were the British on the seas at this point that some officers believed land forces to be optional—the powerful navy could blockade the coast and economically strangle the young nation. The disparity was borne out in the numbers, where even at its peak, the American navy was outgunned by a count of 3,714 to 422.

The colonial response to this obvious threat was initially sketchy. Conceptually, individual colonies still mattered more than the group as a whole, so, starting with Rhode Island, they began to build navies of their own. Rhode Island, which depended heavily on oceanic commerce for its lifeblood, was quite eager for a little payback—for years, the British had made life miserable for its legion of smugglers. The colony tried to talk the Continental Congress into taking the lead on a unified navy, but Congress tabled the measure, coincidentally just a week before Arnold's little Lake Champlain fleet was wiped from the face of the earth.

For his part, George Washington was convinced of the need for ships, going as far as purchasing the schooner *Hannah* with his own money. Outfitted with four small guns and sent to sea from off the coast of Massachusetts on September 2, 1775, the little ship scored a quick win with the capture of a British sloop transporting naval supplies. But as glory goes, that was about it for the *Hannah*. Chased mercilessly by the British, it ran aground barely a month after it was commissioned.

By October 13, 1776, Congress had agreed to the need for a Continental Navy, and on November 4, it purchased the merchant ship *Black Prince* and renamed it *Alfred*, the first ship to fly an early version of the Stars and Stripes, the flag itself hoisted by future American naval hero John Paul Jones. The *Alfred* was soon joined in Philadelphia by the *Cabot, Andrea Doria, Columbus*, and *Providence*. The fleet went charging down the Delaware River, only to be iced in for six weeks by a colonial version of the polar vortex.

The British Navy, depicted here arriving in Jersey in 1776, was far superior to its American counterpart. In fact, some in the British command believed that the Rebels could be defeated without the need for any ground troops whatsoever. Courtesy National Archives.

There would come to be plenty of ships fighting for America, sort of, but most of them were privately owned merchant ships that could make a nice chunk of change on the side by capturing their British equivalents. The way things worked, booty captured by the privateers was split among the crew, making this a far more popular career choice than working on a Navy ship for mere government pay. So among the numerous other problems and indignities suffered by the Continental Navy was a shortage of men who were either willing to sail or knew what they were doing once they'd signed up. It wasn't unusual for new boats to sit idle for lack of a crew. But men of merit did rise to the top—Jones, John Barry, Silas Talbot—although one of these great men was not a man at all, but a boy.

Joshua Barney's grandfather William had been sent to the New World by an uncle in 1695 at the age of fourteen. Ostensibly, this was a generous move on the part of the uncle so that the lad could have the opportunity to seek his fortune and all that, although it's more likely that William's parents had died and the uncle was interested in snagging the boy's inheritance for himself. Whatever, the captain of the ship upon which William sailed was well paid to ensure that the boy didn't step aboard the next vessel returning to Britain. William quickly adapted to the New World and made a fortune of his own, which he passed to a son, William. This son married the heiress Frances Holland Watts, and the couple proceeded to have fourteen children, including Joshua, born in 1759. Spread out on a handsome estate near a community of scattered houses that was going by the name of Baltimore, everything was proceeding well for the Barney family until, lacking television, one of the little tykes was allowed to amuse himself with an old broken and unloaded pistol. While the gun might have indeed been old, in the final analysis it was neither broken nor unloaded, for it went off, mortally wounding father William.

His father taken away "in the meridian of life," as the saying went at the time, young Joshua went to school until he was ten years old, at which point he became convinced he had, his words, "learnt everything the master could teach." At this age, Joshua considered himself ready to go to sea. However, his mother considered differently and sent him to work in a drygoods store in the village. Writing his biography sixty years later, Barney's daughter-in-law rationalized it, "(W)ho that had once conceived a wish to embrace the bold, adventurous, roaming life of a sailor, ever yet contented himself with the dull, lazy, feminine employment of measuring cloth and calico by the yard?" Fortunately for young Barney, the merchant went out of business three months later, and the boy resumed his habit of hounding his mother to allow him to hop aboard a ship. But it was not to be, and he landed in a counting house in Alexandria, Virginia.

Joshua found this to be no more satisfying than retail, and finally, at the age of twelve, he was allowed to go to work on a pilot boat, whose relatively safe duty was to ferry seamen back and forth between their ships and shore. At thirteen, he was apprenticed to Captain Thomas Drysdale, who was in fact his brother-in-law and ran a trading brig, *Sidney,* between Baltimore and Liverpool. Perhaps owing to the family tie, the boy was named second mate, which technically was the ship's third in command, although the odds of him ever being called on to captain the *Sidney* was about the same as the US presidency, through an unlikely series of tragedies, falling to the Speaker of the House.

Over the coming year the ship traversed the ocean, with Barney learning the intricacies of the high seas and putting his counting-house knowledge to work managing the trading books. Three days before Christmas in 1774, the brig sailed from Baltimore bound for Nice (then a province of Sardinia) on the Mediterranean with a valuable load of wheat. Shortly after clearing the Virginia capes, the *Sidney*'s pump well sprang a leak that was beyond the crew's ability to repair. Having to return to Norfolk, Captain Drysdale went off on the first mate with a devastating landslide of profanity, apparently blaming him for dereliction of duty in allowing the leak to develop into such a problem. Believing himself not at fault, the mate didn't take kindly to the insult and walked off the job. So when the *Sidney* was once again seaworthy, she left shore without a first mate, which normally wouldn't have been all that big an issue except that a few days out to sea, Captain Drysdale got sick and died.

Despite all the talk of equality, colonial military advancement depended much on privilege or having friends in high political office. Joshua Barney, who took command of his first ship when he was fifteen, was the exception. Courtesy Library of Congress.

At this point, the eyes of every man in the sizable crew swung to their new boss, fifteen-year-old Joshua Barney. A couple of things that we might have expected to happen, didn't. For one, no one stepped forward to challenge the young man's authority. Why that didn't happen is anyone's guess; but if nineteenth-century accounts are to be believed, where ingenuity and intelligence were concerned, this wasn't exactly the crew of the Starship *Enterprise*. Young as he was, Barney was probably the most qualified person aboard to handle the challenges that would lie ahead.

Second, even with no one to challenge his authority, it might have made sense for Barney to simply turn around and return to Virginia. The repairs to the ship hadn't held, and a difficult journey was at hand even with a captain of significant experience. But in spite of his youth, or perhaps because of it, Barney was determined to deliver the cargo as promised. As if the leak—now bad enough to require a 'round-the-clock bucket brigade—weren't bad enough, a winter gale blew in just as they entered the Mediterranean. Based on its logs, Mary Barney wrote, ". . . the struggling ship heaved and groaned like some living, agonized monster, as she labored to mount the swell—opposing waves at every moment threatened to engulf her in their yawning abyss; and the stoutest heart on board began to beat at each recurring surge with less and less of hope."

Barney had little choice but to put in at Gibraltar where, despite being in a foreign port with no friends and no contacts and as water threatened to ruin the cargo of grain, he managed to secure a loan for repairs. After three months and at a cost of 700 pounds sterling—to be paid out of the profits from the load of wheat—the *Sidney* and her crew were ready for the troubling adventure's final leg.

Unfortunately, their greatest tribulations were yet to come. After arriving in Nice, Barney met with the buyers of the wheat to close the deal. All seemed well and good until the boy returned in ten days to receive payment for his cargo and repay the loan to his creditors (not that they didn't trust the boy, but one of the creditors had come along just to be sure). But the merchants, having consulted their lawyers, were quite full of themselves, having learned that a contract with a minor was not binding. Having discovered this loophole, it was apparent that they intended to take possession of the grain without paying for it. Barney raced back to the ship and ordered the crew to stop off-loading the wheat. For this act of defiance, he was hauled up before the district governor of Nice, who threw him in the dungeon until such time as he would rescind his orders.

The teenager, as only teenagers can, seethed with righteous indignation for a couple of hours in the calaboose before declaring that he had seen the light and would be willing to tell his crew to resume unloading the cargo. The governor granted Barney his release, and once again the boy hurried back to his ship, but instead of releasing the grain, he ran the British colors up the mast and made it clear that any effort to illegally board his ship would be treated as an international incident. The governor made it clear he didn't care about any of that, and sent an armed force to break open the hatches and secure the wheat. Barney responded by ordering his men to retire from the *Sidney* and declaring that "I shall leave my colors flying, that there may be no pretense hereafter of ignorance as to the *nation* to which this insult has been offered."

You could see the wheels turning in the head of the governor's commanding officer, who was the first to have an inkling that the situation might not end well. He protested that it was not his intention to provoke the British government, but by this time Barney was gone. The lad found his creditor, by now something of a friend and mentor, who proposed that they travel to Milan to file a protest with the British Ambassador at the Court of Sardinia. The two crossed the snow-covered Alps on mules (an adventure that was book-worthy in and of itself) and arrived in the company of Britain's Sardinian representative, Sir William Lynch.

The noted diplomat did his work, and in three days, Barney was informed that he would encounter no more tomfoolery out of the governor of Nice. This proved to be an understatement. On his arrival back in the city, his reception from the man who had once called him a "presumptuous stripling" was "ludicrous in the extreme, and Barney," his daughter-in-law wrote, "could scarcely refrain from laughing in his face at his obsequious endeavors to conciliate him . . ." The grain was paid for, the loan was paid off, and the cost of the trip to Milan reimbursed. The governor, literally hat in hand, even offered to compensate Barney for his time spent in prison, an offer the boy refused. The affair of the boy and the governor did not escape the attention of city gossips, and as Barney prepared to return to the colonies, he received a steady stream of well-wishers congratulating him for getting the better of the troublesome bureaucrat.

But the tribulations of this star-crossed journey were not over. Before he could escape the Mediterranean, along with all other nearby vessels, Barney's ship was pressed into duty by the King of Spain as part of a 400-ship armada destined for an attack on Algiers. The attack went so poorly that it became a permanent blot on Spanish naval history, and made Barney all the more happy to return to the port of Baltimore, which he did on October 1, 1775.

If Barney thought his own adventures unbelievable, he was awestruck to hear what had happened in the colonies during his absence. Lexington. Ticonderoga. Bunker Hill. Barney, just three months past his sixteenth birthday, confessed that he "devoured" this reconnaissance with a "greedy ear" and tried his best to contain his "rebellious spirit," since the parties delivering the news were none other than British naval officers who had boarded his ship in the Chesapeake Bay to search for weapons and correspondence.

Since he had been at sea since the age of twelve, the boy-captain had little idea of events that had been driving the colonies to break from the motherland. His biographer records that "When at last he landed, and saw and heard on every hand the din of preparation, and listened to the groups of old and young as they recounted at corners and public places the story of his country's wrongs and the long catalogue of British tyranny and injustice, his heart grew big, and his whole frame dilated—he felt himself already a Commodore."

Since Barney lacked political connections in the Congress and didn't come from old money, no one was going to hand him the rank of commodore just yet. Instead, he settled on sec-ond-in-command for the sloop *Hornet*, where he was ordered to begin recruiting a crew. Desirous of nautical fighters, he did what any recruiter of the time would do: He successfully canvassed the ranks of Maryland's waterfront taverns. Duly staffed, the *Hornet* and sister ship *Wasp* rendezvoused with the *Alfred* et al, and early in 1777 this modest American navy was ready for war. The first mission was to sail to the Bahamas to seize a store of gunpowder, a task that got off to an inauspicious start when a colonial ferry collided with *Hornet,* putting both out of any future fight. The raid itself was a marginal success; the British were able to secret away a majority of the gunpowder, but the Americans did manage to capture a sizable cache of cannon and ammunition.

A private merchant ship purchased by Congress and outfitted for war in 1776, the USS *Lexington* was among the first handful of ships to serve in the Continental navy. She was first captained by John Barry, who along with John Paul Jones is known as the Father of the American Navy. The *Lexington* acquitted herself well for a year and a half before she was captured by the British. Courtesy National Archives.

Yet for every victory, there seemed to be multiple defeats. On the return trip, Barney disguised the *Hornet* as a merchant ship, luring an outgunned British vessel to attack. But just as the ship came in range and Barney was prepared to fire the first gun, the captain, a deeply religious man, called the whole thing off on the intriguing notion that war was no excuse for bloodshed. An enraged Barney threw the lit torch at his head, an act for which he feared he'd be court-martialed. Instead, the shamed captain disappeared into his quarters and was not seen for days. While Barney was gratified to escape discipline, he was pessimistic of becoming a naval officer without any pedigree or friend in a high place to recommend him. Nevertheless, he dispatched himself well in the early days of the war, and his performance did not escape notice.

Following a heroic performance against the British in the Delaware River, Barney was summoned into the presence of the great patriot and war financier Robert Morris, who was serving as president of the Marine Committee. Morris looked Barney over and then presented him with a document, saying, "The committee have heard of your good behavior, Mr. Barney, during the engagement with the enemy in Delaware, and have authorized me to offer you this letter of appointment as a Lieutenant in the Navy of the United States." Joshua Barney was sixteen years old.

Barney did indeed rise to the rank of commodore, and led a daring and adventurous life all the while. And he always remembered his friends. After one pitched battle with a British ship that he had no business winning but did anyway, his men discovered a live sea turtle in the hold with instructions carved in the shell to have it delivered to the table of Lord North. Along with armaments and other spoils, Barney seized the turtle—and had the delicacy shipped to the kitchen of Robert Morris.

Chapter 6
Powdered Wigs to the Rescue

On June 12, 1781, a rowdy and exuberant French legion under Armand Louis de Gontaut, the duc de Lauzun, quit its winter quarters in Connecticut and headed south to reinforce General Washington's beleaguered troops outside of New York City. Lauzun, a conqueror on battlefields and in bedrooms alike, acknowledged in his memoirs that his life had "been made up of . . . strange whims and caprices of fortune." In this he was not alone. Along with tipping the balance in favor of the colonists, the French left behind an epic trail of fascinating stories and legacies, many of which have understandably taken a back seat to the American heroes in the drama.

The contrasts were delicious. Into a land that paid homage to equality, the common man, and raccoon earmuffs, arrived dukes and counts and marquises. This gaily painted calliope of *noblesse oblige* came determined to rescue these poor clodhoppers from themselves and to collect armloads of heroic stories with which to enchant the ladies back at court. Americans were somewhat agape at the Lauzun Legion's white leggings, powder-blue wool coats, and tri-corner hats; the cavalrymen were upholstered in even more elegant fashion that included scarlet breeches laced with gold brocade and hats shaped like plumed Quaker Oats canisters. Their meeting with the raggedy, disheveled native forces would have been like Liberace meeting *Duck Dynasty.*

The Americans and the French got on as well as one would have expected.

The Seven Years' War had started with such promise for the French, but ended in humiliation, their long-held claims in North America that had been so carefully cultivated by Samuel de Champlain gone. War had exhausted the nation, emotionally and financially; yet, if anything, the peace had only hardened their hatred of the British, and they were ready to jump at the first chance at revenge. The American Revolution might not have been seen so much as a good cause as a good excuse. The French, not wishing to be part of another losing cause, dallied until the American victory at Saratoga in 1777, at which point they felt safe in openly supporting the Revolution.

Some 6,000 soldiers under the Comte de Rochambeau arrived in 1780, following an oceanic voyage that had gone poorly at every turn. There was trouble finding ample ships and men, the winds were uncooperative, and a generous passel of goodwill gifts were lost somewhere in the Atlantic. Maybe worst of all, their barrels of wine leaked. Perhaps emblematic of the entire swashbuckling, hellbent-for-leather adventure was Lauzun's right-hand man, Robert Dillon, who just prior to sailing hopped off his boat to mail some letters. And disappeared. He finally dragged himself back to the ship four days later with cutlass wounds to his belly and arms, the result of a hotly fought duel over some perceived insult at the post office. For holding up the whole enterprise, Dillon was only mildly punished.

The advance troops arrived in Newport, Rhode Island, in late summer 1780 to the cheers of no one. Instead of saviors, the French were initially viewed with suspicion (it hadn't been so long ago that the French and Indians had been America's enemy). The streets were empty with only an occasional frowning face peering out from behind a curtain to see what these Frenchmen were about. There was a popular perception that instead of fighting, the French would be preoccupied with fussing with their wigs before dining on frog legs and nightingale tongues. The natives were also underwhelmed with the size of the French force, and it was only after Rochambeau explained to the governor that the main force would be arriving shortly that the people offered up suitable huzzahs and fired off a couple of rockets.

The French under the comte de Rochambeau arrived in Rhode Island in 1780. There was a certain irony to a nation of kings and nobles coming to the assistance a land of commoners and equality. Less than a decade later, France would experience her own revolution. Courtesy National Archives.

If the Americans had reservations, so did the French, who were flabbergasted at the Americans' single-minded pursuit of cash and their propensity to double the going prices on anything their captive audience might want to purchase. Hans Axel, Count von Fersen, a Swede who chose the French military as a career, wrote that "Their greed of money is unequaled: their money is their god; virtue, honor—nothing in the world is of any account but the precious metal." When it came to doing business, the Count complained that the Americans treated them more as enemies than friends. Like many of the outsized personalities and soldiers of fortune who sailed to America's assistance, von Fersen cast a long shadow on the French stage, which at the moment was rife with pent-up energy. France was less than a decade from its own revolution, which would cost royalty and aristocrats their heads and culminate in the horrific Reign of Terror.

One side motive for von Fersen's departure from France was to put to rest rumors that he was sharing a bed with Queen Marie Antoinette, an unpopular native of Austria. The von Fersen affair might have been true or it might have been grist for a rumor mill that insisted the queen was a slut and that King Louis XVI was impotent. Pushed on the subject prior to his departure, von Fersen demurred, quipping that he "left France a free man and unfortunately with no regrets." But, unpopular as the queen might have been, the malaise brewing in France at the time was larger than anything that could be explained away by a foreign queen.

In 1780, the French ministry decided to back up its money and supplies with troops. "As soon as it was made known," wrote Gaston Maugras in a biography of the duc de Lauzun, "this news caused a frenzy of enthusiasm in the French nobility, always eager and valiant." Younger officers who had never known war "could not contain themselves for joy at the thought of reaping glory at last on a field of battle." The best young Frenchmen appealed to King Louis XVI to be sent to America to fight. Never accused of being a great intellect to begin with, Louis apparently failed to put two and two together as he was granting their requests. Monarchs at the time had their differences, but it was certainly unusual for a king to support the cause of a republic. "But it was perhaps even more extraordinary to see the Government sending forth all its young aristocracy to imbibe notions of independence and liberty which they would subsequently import into France," Maugras wrote.

The Americans weren't always sure how to take the French aristocracy, who they assumed would spend their time primping and chasing the ladies. They did both, but they also knew how to fight. Courtesy National Archives.

And as always, along with the born Frenchmen, there were world travelers on the face of the planet who were always spoiling for a fight and seemed to care little about the whos, whys, and wherefores. Such was the band of international desperadoes who came together to form the core of men fighting under the duc de Lauzun.

Lauzun's Legion, wrote Robert A. Selig, "was unconventional to say nothing of undisciplined . . . they accounted for about a sixth of the French forces, but caused about two thirds of the troubles" for Rochambeau. Lauzun's Legion was a fairly representative precursor of the French Foreign Legion that would come along in another fifty years. Only a minority of the Legion were French, the rest coming from no fewer than fifteen assorted nations from one side of Europe to the other. The majority were from Alsace-Lorraine and various other Germanic territories—some would have been Hessian deserters—Selling wrote that they spoke eight languages, but the command was spoken in German, although "by tradition and heritage" members took care to swear in Hungarian.

It was to his credit that Lauzun was able to limit all this commotion to a slow boil and bring them to play a key role in driving the British from American shores.

Born in 1747, the duc de Lauzun was as fascinating as any of the young men who took up arms against the British. The son of a decorated officer, he literally grew up in the lap of King Louis XV's mistress, Madame de Pompadour. At age fourteen he was taken into the bedroom of a female courtier at Versailles, and from that initiation life became an amorous carousel. His memoirs are a nonstop romp from mistress to mistress, with the occasional wickedly funny commentary on the dullard husbands he deceived. The only thing that could distract him from the luxurious life of a professional romantic was the "smell of gunpowder," and he showed interest in military affairs from an early age. An ensign in the French Guards at thirteen and a colonel at twenty, he had the misfortune of coming of age in a rare moment of European peace. An accomplished writer and editor of Madame de Pompadour's letters, Lauzun made a name for himself in military circles by writing a brilliant white paper on British and colonial defenses. He was rewarded with a command that successfully recaptured Fort Saint Louis in Senegal from the British.

The French arrived in America too late in the year to campaign. That was unfortunate since the last thing the Legion needed was time on its hands, both for the legionnaires and anyone they might come in contact with—including each other. With no enemy to fight, one diarist estimated 20 percent of the men became involved in arguments that were embroiled to the point of a duel—including, it almost goes without saying, the intrepid Robert Dillon, who wounded the brother-in-law of the Marquis de Lafayette over a "trivial offense."

The French aristocracy, meanwhile, amused itself by hunting women and squirrels, apparently having more luck with the former, who swooned over the flirtatious young foreigners. When one blushing maiden said she understood him to be married, Lauzun laughed heartily and said, "Married! Yes, but too little—so very little that it is scarcely worth mentioning." Fersen feared, however, that winter in primitive New England would be unbearable. The dandies needed their entertainment and dark months spent without mistresses, banquets, and balls might be more than they could bear.

Worse, as the months passed, no supply ships arrived with food, clothing, and reinforcements. The French ministries of war and naval affairs were in such disarray at the time, and the men in such an array of insubordination, that one officer refused to take a navy command, saying "A degree of daring, of which I am quite incapable, is indispensable for the conduct of a French squadron of ships." The Prime Minister Comte de Maurepas was similarly frustrated when unable to convince the ministries to send the remainder of Lauzun's Legion to America: "I have not been able to achieve what you wish. You had only the king and myself on your side; that is what comes of keeping such low company."

By spring, Rochambeau decided to make do with what he had, and plans were hatched to march to New York and combine forces with General Washington. Lauzun's Legion took the lead and was charged with protecting the army's main force. Washington was duly impressed with the French troops, but it was evident that even their combined forces were not of sufficient strength to dislodge the redcoats from New York. Learning that the French Admiral de Grasse was heading for Chesapeake Bay, the American and French armies moved south. They ended up outside of two towns occupied by General Cornwallis on either side of the York River in Virginia, with Gloucester on the north and Yorktown to the south. The battle lines formed, with Lauzun and his men facing Gloucester, along with the colonial General George Weeden and French Brigadier General Claude Gabriel de Choisy, two men who could not have been less alike. Weeden, Maugras dryly wrote, "was an innkeeper who, in the course of events, had risen to be a general." By most accounts, Weeden was a good man who was not fond of war and, according to Maugras, "still less of Cannon shots." Lauzun, meanwhile, giving perhaps the best description of a military man ever, said Choisy was "a good and gallant man, ridiculously violent, constantly in a rage, always making scenes with everyone, and entirely devoid of common sense." That Lauzun and Choisy took charge of the campaign pleased the innkeeper.

When in early October the time finally came to fight, the Legion proved its worth. It defeated the storied Lieutenant Colonel Banastre Tarleton, a young cavalryman and leader of Tarleton's Raiders, an outfit that was not dissimilar to Lauzun's. With Lauzun and Choisy closing in on Gloucester, and Washington and Rochambeau tightening the noose in Yorktown, Cornwallis surrendered his 7,000 soldiers on October 19, 1871.

Lauzun survived the American Revolution, but not the French, where of course his strong ties to the *Ancien Régime* were not considered to be an asset. He went to the guillotine cool as ever, dining with his executioner and encouraging him to drink up, because a man with such a job must need considerable fortitude. The executioner must have had some trepidation carrying out the task on his new friend, because Lauzun's last words were "We are both Frenchmen; we will do our duty."

CHAPTER 7
Music to the Revolution's Ears

Writing more than a half-century after the conclusion of the Revolution, Alexis de Tocqueville, with some degree of wonder, noted that Americans were devoted to work. The European aristocracy was waning by this time, but even so, labor was widely considered something to be avoided at all costs. The term "workaholic" would have defied definition, and even if the concept could have been understood, the idea of long hours behind a desk or plow as a measure of one's virtue would have been asylum-worthy. At the time of the Revolution, freedom, liberty, and the pursuit of happiness were conceptual—idle crazy talk perhaps, but not particularly threatening. What was threatening to the established order of things were the details. Birth did not determine one's future. Titles didn't matter. Property was up for grabs. One's keep had to be earned.

While this would have terrified a noble, it was music to the ears of a young Frenchman who would be remembered for music but forgotten for a role that was, at least for America's patriotic cause, far more consequential. He was not himself a fighter; he was a playwright who talked Louis XVI into joining the side of the Americans, and secretly sent gunpowder, money, and supplies to desperate American troops.

Pierre-Augustin Caron de Beaumarchais is better known for penning *The Barber of Seville* and *The Marriage of Figaro*. Had he stopped there his career would have been a success, but the breadth of his life—rife with genius, intrigue and perhaps a fillip of irrational exuberance—almost defies belief. The son of a middle-class Parisian watchmaker, Pierre-Augustin Caron grew up in a cacophonous, musical household with five elder sisters. Beaumarchais's biographer, Maurice Lever, writes that "The Caron parents did not scold, so great freedom reigned in the household . . . the Caron tribe was raised culturally well above its social condition, for André-Charles (Pierre's father) was not an artisan like others; watchmaking as a mechanical art required aptitudes going beyond manual skill: knowledge of astronomy, taste and accuracy." The family was steeped in the thoughts and arts of the Enlightenment, and young Pierre's curiosity across a wide spectrum of subjects was insatiable.

At age thirteen, the boy apprenticed with his father with mixed success. Perhaps the breadth of his interests made it hard to focus, but he would abandon the workbench for the harp, and he had a bad habit of filching and reselling the watches he repaired. The time had finally arrived for some tough love, which to his father meant booting him out onto the streets.

He was allowed back only after signing a rigid contract dictating proper behavior.

Watches at the time were less an article of function than fashion. Carved and engraved like metallic lace, accuracy was not paramount; they would likely as not have the bearer a half hour or more early to whatever appointment the owner might have to keep. This nettlesome design flaw was corrected by a new mechanism invented by Pierre-Augustin before he had reached the age of twenty. The slim, accurate design won him an audience with King Louis XV and the business of the fashion-conscious court.

The court of Versailles included a thousand more or less bogus offices that the king sold to the highest bidder. It was by this circumstance that Pierre-Augustin wound up having an affair with the wife of "The Comptroller of the King's Food." The woman, Madeleine-Catherine Aubertin, was able to talk her husband into passing the heady office to Pierre-Augustin. Moreover, within two months the poor cuckold was dead, leaving the former watchmaker not only a new position but a new wife. With his newfound money and status, Pierre-Augustin took the name Beaumarchais, which had no real basis, but sounded good and was a better representation of his new lifestyle.

Within a year, his wife and meal ticket was dead of "putrid fever." Unable to inherit her fortune, Beaumarchais fell into debt, an indignity from which he was spectacularly rescued by the daughters of the King, who had decided they wanted to learn how to play the harp. Thus the erstwhile watchmaker and royal comptroller of food became the man in charge of arranging the king's music. It was this social position that led

Beaumarchais both into state service and into the company of the fabulously wealthy businessmen who patronized the arts.

Suddenly, Beaumarchais found himself with one foot in commerce and the other in the court. Having the ear of the king, he became a valuable lobbyist for the capitalists who were held in such disregard by the nobility. In return for lobbying the king, these men took Beaumarchais under their wing and the watchmaker, writer, and musician added a new skill to his resume—high finance. It was in this vocation that Beaumarchais would be of such use to the American Revolution.

Following a decade of playwriting and rising and falling fortunes, Beaumarchais once again found himself in the service of the king, traveling throughout Europe to put out various brush fires largely related to destroying snarky pamphlets that had been written about one or another of the king's mistresses. It was in this position that Beaumarchais arrived in London on the eve of the Revolution with instructions to put a lid on the amply named Charles-Geneviève-Louis-Auguste-André-Timothée d'Éon de Beaumont.

D'Éon was—where to start?—a soldier in the Seven Years' War, diplomat, spy, and a tremendous actor, who spent thirty-three years of his life as a woman, which allowed him/her to worm his/her way into the court of Empress Elizabeth of Russia for the purpose of agitating against the Habsburgs. (No one was terribly sure of d'Éon's birth gender one way or the other, although for a while a betting pool on the subject was maintained on the London Stock Exchange. D'Éon himself was of no help until physicians examining the corpse following his death in 1810 declared him a male.) Embroiled in the middle of an awkward French power struggle, d'Éon began to publish scandalous accounts of his escapades on the king's behalf, holding back the really juicy stuff in order to ensure that he would be paid handsomely to keep his mouth shut in retirement.

Few people had any luck with d'Éon, so Beaumarchais dealt with the matter as best he could. However, once ensconced in London, Beaumarchais found far bigger fish to fry than a cross-dressing pain in the neck. The watchmaker's son had hacked his way into nobility, it was true, but his sympathies remained with the common man or, more particularly, the common man's right to rise to the top should he be talented enough. So naturally, Beaumarchais was enthralled with the idea of a republic based on the equality and rights of man, and drawn to its cause. The d'Éon problem took a back seat to seeking counsel with Americans who drifted into the city with news of the rebels. With a dramatist's flair, Beaumarchais breathily related the Americans' siege of Boston to the young new king, Louis XVI, who had ascended to the throne on the death of his grandfather in 1774. The twenty-one-year-old monarch was a tough sell. Politics, obviously, would not prove to be his strong point, and he would have been quite happy to be left alone to hunt and dabble in, why not, masonry. Beaumarchais would pepper him with entreaties, to which Louis would generally respond with the royal equivalent of "meh."

Lacking money, clothing, and munitions, Americans meanwhile were afraid the Revolution might die on the vine. At the same time, British officers weren't much more optimistic about their own chances. General John Burgoyne didn't see how Britain could afford to launch an offensive of sufficient size and strength to fight the colonists on their home turf. His idea—and in retrospect, there is a plausible brilliance to it—was to move the British troops to Canada and then sit back and watch as the disparate American political factions devoured each other. The American situation was precariously balanced, and it wouldn't take much of a push on one side or the other to make a real difference in the outcome.

Beaumarchais was the fly on the London wall that catalogued the political winds and reported them back to the French foreign minister Charles Gravier, comte de Vergennes. As such, he was well aware of British dissent toward the hardline colonial policies of George III. At a dinner of British and American radicals, the outspoken London Mayor John Wilkes famously pronounced that "The King of England has long done me the honor of hating me. For my part, I have always done him the justice of despising him. The time has come to decide which of the two has shown better judgment and on which side the wind will cause the heads to fall." Sensing an opportunity, Beaumarchais couldn't get back to Versailles fast enough to tell Vergennes.

But while the minister would come to support Beaumarchais's point of view, he needed to convince the King, who had promised the British that France would stay out of the spat, and who was less than interested in the plight of dirty, liberty-spewing rabble overseas. Beaumarchais finally got to the King with something that the small of mind can readily understand: revenge. Here was a chance to indirectly cripple France's old nemesis, the British, who had treated them so shabbily in the Treaty of Paris.

For the British, it was tremendously expensive to pay for a war that was an ocean away from the motherland, so every livre France snuck into America would have to be matched by Britain by a ratio of ten or even 100 to one. France couldn't be obvious about it, of course, but here was where Beaumarchais's background in finance would pay off. He spared Louis the details—the kid wouldn't have understood the complex transaction anyway—but clandestinely established a sham trading concern named Roderigue Hortalez and Co.

The plot was hatched in conjunction with an American operative in London, Arthur Lee. Lee was prepared to offer a long-term trade agreement with France in exchange for support, which would at least give the King plausible deniability if French and American ships were discovered in each other's harbors. But the agreement went far beyond cash payments and gun-running. Beaumarchais, along with Silas Deane, a Revolutionary (for a time) who set up shop in Paris, brokered one deal after another, procuring ships, signing up free-agent privateers, and dipping into a vast cache of French weaponry that had suddenly and conveniently been declared "surplus."

Through the front company, the French and Spanish funneled money to America, ostensibly as loans or in payment for tobacco. Roderigue Hortalez also supplied the Americans with clothing, muskets, cannon, gunpowder and, most importantly, hope in the otherwise relatively dismal year of 1776. When the Americans won what some consider the turning point of the war at Saratoga, they were already wearing warm clothing shipped from France. The battle itself helped convince the French to overtly support the Americans with troops as well as supplies and paved the way for the arrival of French aristocrats and foreign mercenaries on American shores.

In retrospect, little had gone right for France in the second half of the eighteenth century, and its support of the rebels didn't either. The French finance minister Baron Turgot vehemently opposed the plan, arguing that it would bankrupt the treasury and destabilize the government. But when wars and spies and plots are about, no one listens to finance ministers. Turgot of course was correct; the war drained the French treasury, which was a key component in France's own revolution.

Nor did Beaumarchais—who had always believed that a good arms runner deserved a little something for the effort—profit in the way he had hoped. First, what he understood to be loans were understood by the colonies (or Arthur Lee in particular) to be gifts. Throughout Europe, one hissy fit after another broke out, not over the Revolution itself, but over who would stand to make the most money from it. Lee accused Deane of profiteering. Deane denied the congressional charges, but since gun-runners, privateers, and soldiers of fortune were not in the habit of handing out receipts, his innocence was hard to prove. Nor was there a paper trail from the French government, since the alliance, technically, did not exist prior to France's entry into the war. Caught between the Continental Congress and the French government, it was enough to drive a person over to the side of the Loyalists, which in Deane's case is exactly what happened.

Beaumarchais, for his part, was accused by Doctor Jacques Barbeu-Dubourg (who idolized Ben Franklin, and himself was in line to be the point person for supplying the rebels until Beaumarchais came along) of monopolizing illicit American trade. The two blew up in a meeting with Deane, leading Dubourg to write a whiny letter to Vergennes complaining of Beaumarchais's flamboyance, potential indiscretion, and profiteering. But Beaumarchais had already made it back to Vergennes's office by the time the letter arrived—an amused Vergennes showed it to Beaumarchais, and the two enjoyed a good laugh at Dubourg's expense. Seeing which way the wind was blowing, Dubourg moved to make amends. Beaumarchais was willing, although, understanding the situation perfectly, he quipped that Dubourg was like Turkish women who, prevented by their religion from having affairs, "make love to their husbands for lack of anything better to do."

Unlike the duc de Lauzun, Beaumarchais survived the Terror, largely through the intervention of the angel that seemed to always sit on his shoulder. He was briefly imprisoned, but was released just prior to the September 1792 massacres. He was out of the country on one of his many missions when he was declared an enemy of the Revolution—even though he had in fact tried to supply it with arms—so he was fortunate enough to miss the Reign of Terror that claimed so many other French nobles. He died in 1799 at the age of sixty-seven, to be remembered by history not for war, but for opera. His story could hardly have ended otherwise.

CHAPTER 8
Colonial Cloak and Dagger

George Washington's decisive siege of Yorktown almost didn't happen, because both the Continental Army and the Continental Congress were flat broke. Not only was there no money to pay the troops, there was no money to buy food, forage, munitions, or any of the other of the prodigious supplies needed to maintain an army. The soldiers, after too many years of living on promises, were about at the end of their tether. Washington feared they might be more eager to attack him than the British. Entirely out of chits, he played the only card he had left: He called on Haym Salomon.

If Robert Morris, as he is popularly credited, financed the Revolution, it was Haym Salomon who financed Robert Morris. When luminaries of the time, from the ambassador of Spain to James Madison, were short of funds, Salomon came to their rescue. When the Dutch or French wished to contribute to the American cause, Salomon brokered the bills of exchange.

All told, in today's dollars, he is credited with raising a staggering $8.8 billion for the patriot cause. When Washington came calling, Salomon scraped together the funding needed for the American's final attack. He would be recognized as one of the great icons of American history except that, wrote Michael Feldberg as director of the America Jewish Historical Society, "He operated within the context of a society, and an age, that considered all Jews as Shylocks and money grubbers."

Haym Salomon began his career as a spy, but after being twice captured decided to retire to the less stirring job of financier, when he became the Revolution's chief fundraiser. Courtesy National Archives.

But before all his financial heroism, Salomon was a spy. Twice he was captured by the British. The first time was in 1776 when the British took New York City. Salomon's knowledge of several foreign languages saved him—he was used as an interpreter for the Hessians and talked a goodly number of them into deserting to the American side. The second time, he was sentenced to death, but escaped by greasing the palm of a guard. Having spent enough time behind enemy lines to last a lifetime, he prudently fell back on his financial roots for the duration of the war.

Nathan Hale gets all the ink in Revolutionary spy annals, but no less an authority than the CIA says that Hale "is probably the best known but least successful American agent in the War of Independence." Hale was filled with passion, but outside of that, he "had no training experience, no contacts in New York, no channels of communication, and no cover story to explain his absence from camp—only his Yale diploma supported his contention that he was a Dutch schoolmaster." He was quickly captured and went to the gallows on the same day as Salomon's initial arrest.

It might save time and space to simply name everyone in the Revolutionary War who was not a spy. For every Nathan Hale and John André, there were literally dozens if not hundreds of people involved in more pedestrian grunt work, infiltrating enemy lines, passing encoded notes, and planting false information. British and Americans alike were shocked to discover that their most trusted agents were doing the enemy's bidding. Benjamin Franklin's secretary in France, Edward Bancroft, copied down everything the great statesman wrote and dropped it in a hollow boxwood tree for his British handlers. Because of that, King George knew that a Franco-American alliance had been signed two days after it happened and weeks before news reached the colonies.

John André will forever be branded as the man who facilitated Benedict Arnold's defection, but he was such an interesting, talented, and likable man that even Washington was sorry to see him hanged. Courtesy National Archives.

Sometimes the armies on both sides all but asked for their secrets to be revealed. Men took no precautions when discussing battle plans in front of women, feeling that the little ladies were too naive to understand the language of war. Women were more than happy to bat their eyelashes in front of the nice generals and then make off with their most guarded plans. Same with slaves; Cornwallis's jaw hit the floor when he discovered it was a trusted servant and runaway slave who'd given away his secrets and helped the Americans and French capture Yorktown.

As would be expected in the days that predated electronics, the methods were not terribly sophisticated, and often sound more like techniques employed by nine-year-old boys in their secret clubhouses. Invisible ink was popular. Fake love letters would disclose a far less amorous message when exposed to heat. So would the blank pages in an almanac, ledger, or other cheap notebook. Page masks were popular, too, although rigging them up must have been quite a chore. The mask itself was a sheet of paper with a shape—like a snowman, for example—cut out of the center. When the mask was placed over a page of writing, the words that appeared through the cutout would have a far different meaning than the full page. The letters and masks were delivered separately in case they fell into enemy hands.

Of course, the couriers themselves could be problematic. Some would take top-secret correspondence and race straight to the enemy officers, who would carefully break the seal, read the letter, and then reseal it with hot wax before it was taken to its intended recipient.

Many people spied and many spies were caught—sometimes with deadly, sometimes with humorous, but usually with fascinating result.

In 1777, three British generals were stirring the New England pot: William Howe, Henry Clinton, and John Burgoyne, all three of whom had arrived in Boston in 1775, with Howe destined to become commander in chief.

Howe had the résumé. He was, in fact, the illegitimate uncle of George III, his grandmother having logged time as the mistress of George I. He helped run the French out of Canada in the French and Indian War, retained a seat in Parliament, and was promoted to Major General at the age of forty-three. And if he was a skirt chaser, he was at least a dignified skirt chaser, not one of those snickering French party animals. But he accepted the assignment to quell the rebellion reluctantly, stating that he had been "ordered and could not refuse." In Boston, he was the technical winner of the Battle of Bunker Hill, but was so badly stung by the tenacious colonists that he never seemed to regain his mojo.

Nipping at Howe's heels was the irritating but gifted Clinton, so paranoid that he made hand-written duplicates of every slip of paper that crossed his desk, from letters to restaurant receipts. Clinton was ever urging Howe to advance against Washington, advice Howe followed only occasionally.

Caught in the middle—or, more accurately, hung out to dry—was the dashing gambler and playwright Burgoyne, who drew up plans to split the colonies in two. He was to march south through the Champlain Valley from Montreal, while Howe marched north from New York City and Lieutenant Colonel Barry St. Leger marched east through the Mohawk Valley from Ontario. All would meet up in the vicinity of

Albany. The American forces caught in between would be crushed, the colonies split, and the rebellion defeated. It was a likely enough plan, had someone only bothered to tell Howe. To this day no one is certain where the break in communication came, but Howe was intent on heading not north but south, where he was ultimately successful in capturing the capital city of Philadelphia, to which we will return in a moment.

British General John Burgoyne was a handsome man of many talents, which may have inspired a bit of jealousy in General William Howe, who failed to come to his aid in Saratoga. Or maybe Howe just didn't get the memo. Courtesy National Archives.

Burgoyne was not so fortunate. While he was able to retake Fort Ticonderoga in the summer of 1777, trouble was already brewing. The Loyalists he was expecting to join his ranks never materialized. Supplies were running low, and units dispatched on foraging missions were clobbered by shadowing Americans. This caused the Native Americans in his ranks to lose interest and disappear into the forest. By now he had an inkling from coded messages from Clinton that Howe's army could not be counted on, meaning the mission would be up to Burgoyne and St. Leger. But out west things weren't working out well for the British either, where a game of subterfuge was about to break out.

St. Leger correctly believed that there was only one mildly worrisome trouble spot between Lake Ontario and the planned rendezvous with Burgoyne, that being the ratty, lightly defended Fort Stanwix, which controlled an important carry that linked the waters of the Atlantic with those of the Great Lakes. What St. Leger didn't know was that the Americans anticipated his move, and that in the spring of 1777, General Philip Schuyler, commander of the northwestern theater, had sent Colonel Peter Gansevoort's Third New York Regiment to fix up and defend Fort Stanwix. So the fort had as many as 800 men, instead of the sixty St. Leger was expecting. And even as the British laid siege to the fort, General Benedict Arnold was drawing near with a relief force of 700 men.

To compensate, St. Leger mustered Indians and Tories in the Mohawk Valley. One night a handful of soldiers, Indians, and Tory spies were strategizing at the home of a local Loyalist. A British officer was in the middle of a stirring recruitment speech when an armed detachment of colonists burst through the door and captured the lot.

In an old history of the fort, W. Max Reid wrote that "Among the Tories who were captured and sentenced to death was a half-witted fellow named Han Yost Schuyler. Having been associated with the Indians on the frontier by force of circumstance and inclination, he was regarded by the savages with the superstitious reverence that they have for simple-minded people. His mother, an old half-gypsy creature, and his brother Nicholas implored General Arnold to spare his life, but Arnold was obdurate."

The old gypsy became "almost frantic in her grief," and after giving the matter a little more thought, Arnold finally proposed terms on which he would pardon her son. Arnold's terms were a cloak and dagger masterpiece. First, he had the hapless spy's coat and hat hung from a tree and shot full of holes. Next, he told Han Yost to spread the word through the Indian camps that 3,000 American troops were closing in on the fort's gates.

Han Yost might have been simple, but with his life in the balance he proved to be a superb actor. He told his tale to the awestruck Indians, and when they asked how many men the Americans had, Han Yost raised his finger skyward and pointed to the leaves on the trees. The Indians concluded that the British planned to use them as cannon fodder in the face of this overwhelming force, and with that in mind, they decided to get while the getting was good. St. Leger tried to talk them out of it and even resorted to the European ace in the hole where Native American negotiations were concerned—firewater. Given the choice between sobriety and slaughter, however, the Indians chose the former.

Their disorganized flight naturally caught the attention of the British regulars, who received just enough of an answer to their queries to decide that they might too be interested in a headlong flight to the safety of their boats back on Lake Oneida. According to Reid's account, they began to outdo the Indians in this regard, to the point that the Indians—still steamed at the idea that the British had set them up—began to tackle the retreating soldiers and take possession of their gear. They even accelerated the donnybrook by shouting "They're coming, they're coming" into the ears of the retreating redcoats. St. Leger later said that Indians became more formidable to his men than the enemy they had expected to do battle with. "Such was their haste," Reid wrote, "that they left their tents, baggage, and artillery behind, and the bombardier was left asleep in the bomb battery! When he awoke he found himself alone, the sole representative of the besieging army. The Indians continued their cry, at intervals, 'They are coming! They are coming!' behind the fleeing Tories, and thus amused themselves all the way to Oneida Lake."

As obscure as this action in central New York might seem today, it was crucial to Burgoyne's interests in the summer of 1777, as one more source of reinforcements went by the boards. Even worse, on July 17, 1777, General Howe wrote to Burgoyne, congratulating him on the big win at Ticonderoga, but sending his regrets that he in all likelihood would be unable to participate in the festivities in upstate New York, per Burgoyne's grand design: "Washington is waiting our motions here, & has detached Sullivan with about 2500 men, as I learn, to Albany. My intention is for Pennsylvania where I expect to meet Washington, but if he goes Northw.d contrary to my (expectations) and you can keep him at Bay, be assured I will soon be after him to relieve you."

The news, which was bound to be a disappointment to Burgoyne, was written on two long threads of tissue paper rolled up and stuffed into a quill-tipped pen and delivered by a British operative. Letters written on these easily hidden paper strips was a favorite technique of British spies. Along with quills, the missives could be secreted in hollowed buttons or silver balls with varying degrees of success. One such letter from General Henry Clinton to Burgoyne was of such little consequence in terms of content that it was hardly worth the trouble—except that it wound up being quite consequential to the spy, Daniel Taylor, who carried it.

Understanding that Burgoyne was now in serious trouble, Clinton ascended the Hudson River valley himself, hoping that he could take the pressure off the northern army, which he reckoned should by now be nearing Albany. Clinton captured two forts along the way, by the names of Montgomery and Clinton. (The last artillery shot from the Americans as they fled Fort Clinton was said to be fired not by a man, but by a burly red-headed woman who had refused to leave her husband's side when he went off to fight; this same woman would cement her legend a year later at the Battle of Monmouth where, the story goes, her tireless efforts to get water to the troops earned her the nickname Molly Pitcher.)

Molly Pitcher, the water-toting heroine of Monmouth, probably existed in some form or another, although her legend didn't really gather steam until the mid-1800s. She was likely a compilation of the women who would hang around the army for various reasons. Courtesy National Archives.

Both forts secured, Clinton happily fired off a note to Burgoyne that had the tone of a vacationer's post card from the Florida Keys: "*Nous y voici* [here we are] and nothing between us but (American General Horatio) Gates. I sincerely hope this little success of ours may facilitate your operations . . ."

The letter was written on a snippet of tissue three inches square, stuffed into a silver ball the size of a cranberry, and entrusted to Taylor on October 10 with the orders to swallow it if he were unfortunate enough to be captured. He'd been on the road for a few hours when he came across a band of redcoats at the village of New Windsor who demanded to know his business. Taylor said he was carrying a message for Clinton, an announcement that did not seem to cause any discernible reaction among the soldiers, who told him that Clinton was just up the road and that they would grant him an immediate audience so he could deliver the missive in person. This of course confounded Taylor, who had been riding his horse for some time and was certain that he'd left his boss far in the rear view mirror.

What the courier failed to appreciate was that one of the forts the British had just taken—he might have known by the name—had been commanded by the American governor George Clinton who was, sadly for Taylor, no relation to Sir Henry. George Clinton had retreated north after abandoning the fort and was at the moment retrenching to defend against Henry Clinton's march north. Where those red coats came from remains something of a mystery, although it was suspected that the Americans had captured them in some past battle. Anyway, the instant Taylor saw which Clinton he was dealing with, he nearly collapsed at the combination of coincidence and bad luck that had led to his discovery. And his luck didn't improve. In the general confusion he unobtrusively gulped down the silver ball, but someone noticed and summoned the camp surgeon, who gave the spy a strong dose of tartar emetic, and up came the ball. The intrepid Taylor snatched the ball from amid the ick and swallowed it again. The commander shrugged and said it was all the same to him—he'd just have Taylor hanged and cut the ball out of his gut. On hearing this, Taylor voluntarily grabbed the bottle of the purgative and chugged a second dose.

In the end it didn't matter. Taylor was hustled to the nearby town of Hurley, where in no time whatsoever he was tried as a spy, convicted, and hanged from an apple tree. The very next day, Burgoyne surrendered to the Americans at Saratoga.

In hindsight, it is fairly clear that Howe had little interest in assisting Burgoyne in the first place. And while it might have been miscommunication, it's also possible, maybe even likely, that Howe was ill-disposed to carry water for a plan that would win laurels for a professional rival. Or he might have simply thought his plan to focus on General Washington and Philadelphia would bring a quicker end to the war.

So, whatever the reason, instead of marching north up the Hudson, Howe's army could be found the late spring of 1777 performing a series of wounded-quail maneuvers, trying to tempt Washington—who had entrenched his men in the western New Jersey mountains—into abandoning his safe position and attacking on ground that favored the British. But Washington's spies confirmed Howe's true intentions, and the American general stayed put. So Howe sailed his army down the Atlantic coast and then up the Chesapeake Bay to present-day Elkton, Maryland. From there he marched north, where he outmaneuvered Washington's forces at Brandywine Creek, in a battle that ironically enough was fought around a meeting house filled with pacifist Quakers who were holding midweek services.

Washington almost lost his army that day. Only some late-afternoon heroics held off the British advance long enough for the bulk of the American army to escape. But for Howe, the path was mostly clear to Philadelphia, a city he occupied on September 26, exactly three weeks before Burgoyne, his hoped-for reinforcements having never arrived, surrendered his army at Saratoga.

The Philadelphia that Howe captured had a weird vibe. The British had hoped that Philadelphians would rally to the Loyalist cause, but what they found was a city that was three-quarters women and children. It was true that there were loyal elements in Philadelphia, and it was also true that many had quite had their fill of quarrelsome and overzealous founding fathers. But the British had not ingratiated themselves on their march north. While looting was decreed to be a capital offense, even the threat of severe punishment was not enough to prevent soldiers from running roughshod over the local populace. Then there was the unfortunate Paoli Massacre just prior to Philadelphia's capture, in which an American division under the command of the temperamental "Mad Anthony" Wayne was surprised by a British force less than half its size.

Sometimes intelligence in colonial times was sophisticated and sometimes it wasn't. The British certainly had spies acting on their behalf outside of Philadelphia, but here it was just as likely that Wayne's position was given away in simpler fashion. The massacre, or battle, was named after the nearby Paoli Tavern, which in turn had taken its name from a Corsican bandit. Military decorum then wasn't what it is today, and in all likelihood soldiers from both armies met and chatted with each other while downing a gill or two of rum. However it happened, the British knew just where to find the Americans, and they burst upon the patriot camp at 10:00 p.m. with bayonets fixed. (Their guns had been disabled to prevent an errant shot that would give away their position.) While American casualties were in all honesty quite light, the bayonet thrusts led to a surplus of blood and guts, which American propagandists willingly used to promote the image of a massacre. So for a variety of reasons, the British soldiers who entered the largest city in the colonies discovered a populace that was clearly having some misgivings about their arrival.

Along with the women and children living in Philadelphia was a healthy population of Quakers, who not only despised war but also parties, drinking, gambling, costumes, dancing, and public excess. Unfortunately for them, as Howe's army settled in for the winter, the commander and his men looked forward to several months of parties, drinking, gambling, costumes, dancing, and public excess. About the only thing that might have comforted a good Quaker was that Howe seemed to have little inclination to fight.

This was the infamous winter of 1777–78, when the Americans suffered miserably at Valley Forge, twenty miles outside of Philadelphia. Of the 12,000 men stationed there, 2,500 died of disease, starvation, exposure, or a combination of the three. Howe would come to be roundly criticized for not wiping this motley band of armed skeletons from the face of the earth in early 1778, but at the time winter campaigns were not the sort of thing that an officer and a gentleman did. Plus, Howe always seemed to do the bare minimum to fulfill the requirements of a commanding officer, furthering speculation that he had his doubts about the validity of the war.

All that aside, the wealthy Loyalists in the city gave Howe a hearty welcome, and the general seemed not to notice or care about the hardening eyes peering at him from the ranks of the Quakers and middle-class artisans. Before he settled in completely, however, he decided to take one more stab at dealing a mortal blow to the Americans prior to the Christmas holidays. It was designed to be a surprise attack, and throughout the campaign, Howe had been quite good at keeping his movements a secret—to the point that even some of his own officers didn't know what he was up to.

This time, his plans were leaked, not by a traditional spy network but by a diminutive Quaker nurse named Lydia Darragh. Darragh was born in Ireland and rode a wave of immigration from the British Isles to the New World some seventy-five years after William Penn had founded his haven for those who followed the Quaker faith. Her husband was a teacher and she was a midwife and mortician.

By colonial standards, she was getting on in years when the Revolution came almost literally to her doorstep in the form of General Howe, who moved into a large home across the street. Howe knew his neighbors were Quakers, and perhaps let his guard down more than he should, since Friends were theoretically neutral. More than theoretically, actually— a letter written at the Society of Friends' annual meeting for dissemination among all its members ordered members in no uncertain terms to stay out of the war. This was certainly in keeping with religious philosophy, but it was also economically convenient, since many Quakers had built substantial wealth that war threatened.

But while most Quakers adhered to the letter, there were younger Friends who felt they owed the government something for fighting on their behalf. One of these was Lydia's son Charles, who had become an officer in the Continental Army. Howe wouldn't have understood the distinction of these "Fighting Quakers," nor would he have supposed that the old lady across the street was herself part of the patriotic mix. Since the British occupation, Lydia had used her proximity to Howe to pick up tidbits of information, which were secretly sent to Washington in the hollowed buttons of people traveling out of the city—including Lydia herself.

So she likely could hardly believe her luck when Howe's men came knocking on her door in early December, saying they were commandeering her house for a council of war. She and her husband were initially ordered out of the home, until Lydia struck up a conversation with an officer with a strong Irish accent and a family name that was the same as hers. The two turned out to be second cousins, and the newly discovered relative was able to convince Howe that Lydia and her husband would be of no threat if allowed to remain in the comfort of their own home.

The night of the strategy session, the couple were ordered to bed early. Lydia feigned sleep and then tiptoed to the room over the parlor, where she heard plans of the surprise attack at Whitemarsh. The meeting over, she hustled back to her bedchamber. The next morning she received permission from the British command to cross army lines in pursuit of a sack of flour. There are a couple of differing accounts of what transpired next, but the patriot statesman Elias Boudinot, who was responsible for screening captured soldiers at the time, recorded in his journal that he had just finished his afternoon meal at the Rising Sun Tavern outside of the city, when "a little poor looking insignificant Old Woman came in & solicited leave to go into the Country to buy some flour."

Boudinot started asking her some routine questions, and as he did she pressed a grimy needlebook into his hand. Since the officer had not intended to do any sewing that day, he correctly suspected it might be serving some other function. Sure enough, in the last pocket he found a rolled up scrap of paper advising that "Genl Howe was coming out the next morning with 5,000 men, 13 pieces of cannon, baggage wagons, and 11 Boats on Waggon Wheels."

The account is problematic, as it isn't a perfect match to the Lydia Darragh story, leading some to question how much of either narrative is in fact accurate. It's hard to know for certain, but the clues point to the theory that a civilian woman whose identity remains open to debate saved the American army at Whitemarsh. Like many similar stories and legends, the truth is not easily discovered, because spies who left strong documentation of their work didn't stay spies very long. Not live ones, at least.

CHAPTER 9

Where the War Was Won

Frustrated with one holdup and snafu after another in
the northeast in the early days of the war, British General Henry Clinton decided to sail from New York to South
Carolina. Having failed to quickly extinguish the rebellion
from the top down, Clinton would land in the American
South and conquer the continent from the bottom up.

So open was the British general with his plans that the colonists thought it must be a trick. Washington ordered General
Charles Lee to shadow Clinton who, true to his word, showed
up with the British navy off the Charleston coast in the early
spring of 1776. There to greet him, in what was had to be
regarded (knowing now what we didn't know then) as an omi-
nous sign for the British, was Christopher Gadsden, designer
of the yellow "Don't Tread On Me" flag featuring a crudely
drawn coiled snake. There too was South Carolina President

John Rutledge, the man who talked the Continental Congress out of abolishing slavery, and the tightly wound Colonel William Moultrie.

William Moultrie ignored the orders of Continental Army General Charles Lee, which enabled him to defeat the first British attempt to take Charleston, South Carolina. Moultrie split his time between politics and battle, and walked a fine line between heroics and atrocities; in 1775 he led a raid that resulted in the killing of fifty runaway slaves. Courtesy National Archives.

Clinton was to discover, both sooner and later, that he had seriously underestimated the American South. So was Cornwallis, who through his career mastered the Native Americans, French, Irish, and East Indians, but had no answer for the people of the Carolina backcountry.

More battles in the Revolution were fought in South Carolina than in any other colony. In another eighty-five years, the "fire eaters" in Charleston would be blamed for inciting the Civil War. But if the Palmetto State gets the blame for tearing the nation asunder, it certainly deserves credit for establishing the nation in the first place.

Yet this was a colony where the lines of battle were not clearly drawn. You almost get the sense that if the Revolution hadn't come along they would have found something else to fight about, since preexisting hatreds already ran deep, although not in any predictable pattern. British intelligence indicated that South Carolina had more Loyalists than could be found in other colonies. This was accurate but not particularly useful information, since allegiances could turn on a whim. A man's hated enemy could become an ally in a heartbeat if he discovered an enemy he hated even more.

Somewhat typical was the case of Loyalist Alexander Chesney, who emigrated in 1768 from County Antrim in Ireland to South Carolina's Pacolet River, where in 1776 as a nineteen-year-old he was guiding Tory refugees and hiding them in his home. The Whig party that was populated by the patriots caught young Chesney in the act, threw him in jail for a few days, and then gave him a choice of fighting for the rebels or standing trial for aiding the enemy.

Rather than risk the business end of a rope, Chesney chose to fight for the rebels and in fact was quite content doing so, particularly as his outfit went up against the British-allied Indians, for whom settlers on the frontier would have had little use. He remained with the rebels until Clinton returned to the Carolinas in 1780, at which point he switched back to the Loyalist cause. Chesney fought in a dizzying number of conflicts, but in between dust-ups still managed to take a bride, farm his land, and sell wagonloads of produce in Charleston.

Paradoxically, in the popular annals of the American ideal it was generally the men of privilege, wealth, and power in the coastal low country who were the patriots, and the hardscrabble independent sort on the frontier who stayed loyal. A loose explanation is that the British taxes and impositions on trade threatened to stunt the planters' and merchants' ability to make money, while the pioneers saw the British as their protector against Indian attack. (It was also not uncommon for upper-crust colonists in the low country to be deeply in debt to British merchants, debts they wrongly supposed they might not be liable for anymore if they won the war.)

As is always the case, there was no small amount of jealousy and resentment on the part of the upland poor directed at the coastal wealthy. If coastal Carolinians felt they weren't represented in Britain, upland Carolinians felt they weren't represented in their own colony.

Those were the explanations that made some degree of sense. But John W. Gordon, writing in his book *South Carolina and the America Revolution: A Battlefield History*, notes that logical divisions did not always hold: "No single determination of class, section, political ideology or religious affiliation easily explains how the sides chose themselves. The war split communities, districts and families and set the fragments against each other. Fought for the larger purpose of supporting one or the other of the two sides, it was fought also to settle old scores or to best rivals. Payback took the form of looting, physical violence and outright execution of those who fell into the wrong hands."

To the British and their sense of order, this all but caused their heads to explode. In Pennsylvania, Presbyterians were pretty dependable enemies of the King, so the British ran roughshod over Presbyterian communities in the South, unaware that in South Carolina these communities had, if anything, leaned toward the British, since the Carolina government used their hard-earned tax dollars to underwrite the Episcopal Church to which they did not belong. Consequently, inaccurate British assumptions lost them what would have otherwise been natural allies. The British also seemed not to understand that their Cherokee allies would wind up costing them dearly. Settlers who looked to the British for protection from the Indians were astounded that the British and Cherokee were now on the same side. This switched the allegiance of more than a few.

As always seemed to be the case in the white man's wars, the Native Americans wound up choosing the losing side, and soon the Cherokee were forced to retreat to the south, as the frontiersmen used the Revolution as an excuse to take out decades of frustration against their Indian antagonists through unspeakable atrocities and wholesale slaughter.

In short, it was a mess that the British were about to step into. They would have their victories to be sure, but if the term "herding cats" was ever applicable, it was here.

Not even the Continental Army itself was entirely safe from South Carolina's charms. When the British first arrived on the Carolina coastline in the spring of 1776, the patriots were in the process of throwing up a log and sand fort at the entrance to the Charleston harbor. Washington's man, General Charles Lee, didn't like the looks of the forward position and ordered Colonel Moultrie to abandon the fort and regroup closer to town. Moultrie thanked the colonial commander for his suggestion, which he summarily ignored. This caused the predictable cries by Lee of insubordination and the intervention of Rutledge, who sternly told Moultrie he was to obey the commands of General Lee unless he didn't want to.

Moultrie consequently stayed at the fort, which proved to be the right move. One week before the nation officially declared its independence, the British opened up on the position with a fleet that boasted 300 guns. It was of little use. This "slaughter pen" of a fort, as Lee had called it, boasted some unique attributes. One, cannonballs, which typically do considerable damage as they bound along the ground, were entirely swallowed up in the soft sand when they landed. Second, the fort had been constructed of spongy palmetto logs, which make bad lumber but good forts because the cannon balls bounced off the walls, doing no more damage than a rock hammer on a foam peanut.

The result was a patriot victory in the Battle of Sullivan's Island, which encouraged the Americans to declare independence and discouraged the British from bothering the South for another three years.

They would eventually return, however, and this time with a vengeance. The British Royal Army didn't get to be the British Royal Army by taking quarter from a stack of palmetto logs. In December of 1779, with 14,000 soldiers—a tremendous army for the time—and ninety ships, Sir Henry Clinton sailed for South Carolina. The siege of Charleston began on April Fools Day 1780, and with efficient military precision, the British captured the city in little more than a month, along with 5,000 American troops.

Taking charge of the mop-up duty going forward would be Lord George Cornwallis, who had done well against George Washington in New York, but allowed his American counterpart to outfox him in New Jersey to much hooting from the British peanut gallery. Prior to sailing back north, Clinton all but took Cornwallis by the hand and turned him loose on the outskirts of town with orders not to mess this up.

The British generals tended to snipe at each other like passive-aggressive old biddies over a game of bridge, and Cornwallis, a study in boring competence, responded to this snarky pep talk by relaying the news of battles in the South to Clinton months after the fact, when he bothered to mention them at all.

For a British officer accustomed to battlefield formula and to straight-line logistics, nothing could have been worse than the swamps, forests, and Indian trails of South Carolina. Here, the decorated Earl would run into characters with monikers that included the Swamp Fox, the Carolina Gamecock, and the Overmountain Men.

Nor were these buckskinned varmints limited to the male of the species—women frequently played storied roles that resonated through the generations. One of the more colorful was Nancy Morgan Hart, an unspeakably picturesque woman who stood six feet tall with a shock of red hair, crossed eyes, freckles, and a complexion wracked by smallpox. The white man's nickname for her was a rather disappointing "Aunt Nancy"; the Indians more accurately nailed it, calling her "Wahatche," which translated into "Woman of War." Hart and her husband Benjamin migrated south through the Carolina backcountry, and eventually settled along the Broad River across the line in Wilkes County, Georgia.

Tales of Ms. Hart abound, as her story resembles that of a female Davy Crockett, terrorizing Indians, arm-wrestling bears, and whatnot. But much of her story hardly needs to be embellished. Rough as she might have been—her temper and profanity were legend—her husband's side of the family was more refined and would include such notables as Henry Clay and Missouri Senator Thomas Hart Benton.

Hart's hatred for Loyalists was almost enough to warp time. She and her daughter Sukey were apparently alone at the family cabin one day when a half-dozen Tories showed up in search of a troublesome rebel. Hart pleaded ignorance, which fooled no one, and in an ill-advised act of attempted coercion, one of the Tories shot and killed the woman's prized turkey and ordered Hart to cook it for the men.

Outwardly compliant, inwardly seething, Hart seated them around the table and opened up a jug of hooch, which the men passed back and forth, getting tipsier and less cognizant of current events by the minute. Hart used this time to discreetly slip the men's muskets one by one out to Sukey through a gap in the cabin wall. When the Tories finally noticed what was going on and jumped to their feet, she leveled a gun barrel in their direction and ordered them to freeze. Due to her severely crossed eyeballs, the men were not entirely clear on specifically whom she was aiming at, and one who felt himself safe lunged for the bony redhead. Sadly for him, he was indeed the one she had in her sights and she dropped him on the spot. A second Tory who dared test her marksmanship suffered a similar fate.

Alerted to the unfolding drama by Sukey, Hart's husband and several other men soon burst on the scene to find Hart in full control. Consistent with backcountry war protocol, the men thought the Tories should be shot on the spot. Hart wanted to draw out their misery, however, and insisted that they be hanged, which they were. The legend has many variations, but its overall veracity was lent some credibility in 1912 when a railroad construction crew unearthed a neat row of six skeletons lined up in a grave near the old Hart cabin.

Such was the venom the British were dealing with. Worse, Cornwallis was learning that the massive Loyalist army, said to be awaiting orders in the southern hills and hollows, simply didn't exist. Or if it had, its adherents had switched sides or simply faded into the background when they saw who was gaining the momentum. And for all the people who strongly supported one side or the other, at the time of the Revolution perhaps half the population had no preference at all and simply wanted to be left alone.

All that said, the British southern strategy in 1780 looked as if it might just work. They had taken Savannah in late 1778 and Charleston a year later. Having been left in charge by Sir Henry Clinton, Cornwallis unleashed his most venomous weapon, the daring twenty-five-year-old cavalryman Banastre Tarleton. Tarleton has remained a controversial figure right into modern times. His most incendiary nicknames, "The Butcher" and "Bloody Ban," weren't assigned to him until a biography written in 1952.

Tarleton played a key role in a southern American storyline that the British were thugs who, if they won, would make bloodthirsty overlords. The British themselves contributed to the image by threatening violence and retribution against all who failed to come over to their side. Both sides engaged in atrocities, especially in the backcountry, but the Americans seemed to be better at parlaying British outrages into hostility toward the British cause.

Tarleton's reputation was sealed, oddly enough, in May of 1780 with the death of his horse. Toward the end of the month, Tarleton's Raiders, 150 strong, were riding furiously in pursuit of a Colonel Abraham Buford and his Virginia regiment of 350 soldiers of the Continental Army, who were making their escape from Charleston following the successful British siege.

The brutal young cavalry officer Banastre Tarleton was the devil
incarnate to rebel forces during the Revolution. The Americans
said Tarleton's men massacred their soldiers after a flag of truce
had been waved. The British said it was all a misunderstanding.
Courtesy National Archives.

Burford was nearing the North Carolina line when he received a missive from Tarleton demanding his surrender. Buford's council of war determined that to surrender while in possession of a larger force would be ignoble, but that they lacked the firepower to stand and fight. Consequently, they simply ignored Tarleton's missive and continued their march.

On May 29, Tarleton overtook the retreating Continentals and did so much initial damage that Burford saw no alternative but to raise the white flag. At some point—the exact timing is sketchy—Tarleton's horse was struck by a musket ball and went down. In the smoke of battle, Tarleton's men initially believed their commander had been shot, and that he had been shot even as the deceitful Continentals were waving a flag of truce. Their response was swift and they fell on Buford's men with fresh anger, or as Tarleton put it later, with "a vindictive asperity not easily restrained."

The Continentals, for their part, thought they had just surrendered and asked for quarter, or mercy, the acceptance of which was more or less a formality. As such, they were both puzzled and terrified when the British renewed the attack. Without orders to the contrary, the regiment put up little or no resistance to the attack, and the resulting bloodbath became known as the Waxhaws Massacre. (Except of course to the British, who assigned it to history as the Battle of Waxhaws Creek.)

The white flag had its bearer shot out from under it. For fifteen minutes after the final shot of the battle, British cavalrymen wandered the battlefield, plunging their bayonets into any fallen American who was still twitching. Most famously, two British soldiers came across the prone figure of a Virginian by the name of John Stokes.

Stokes had fought bravely. He was engaged in parrying one of Tarleton's dragoons when a second horseman whipped his sword at Stokes, severing his right hand. From there, according to a 1902 history by Edward McCrady, "He was assailed by them both, and instinctively attempting to defend his head with his left arm, was hacked in eight or ten places from the wrist to the shoulder and a finger cut off. His head was laid open almost the whole length of the crown to the eyebrows and after he fell he received several cuts on the face and shoulders."

Left for dead, he nevertheless attracted the notice of another passing soldier, who sneeringly asked if he expected quarter. Stokes responded, "I have not and do not mean to ask it; finish me off as soon as possible." Being in an agreeable mood, apparently, the soldier twice thrust his bayonet through the poor soul and walked away. Remarkably, Stokes survived and in 1790 was named the first federal judge to be seated in the United States District of Western North Carolina. But what the British military could not do, the American judiciary could; Stokes was dead within three months of his appointment.

With Buford—who would retire to bluegrass country, where he helped found the Kentucky horse-racing industry—out of the picture, the Continental Army no longer had a presence in South Carolina. The future of the Carolinas and the nation would be up to civilian militia.

The Continentals did make one last brief push into the state at the important crossroads town of Camden, but Cornwallis got wind of the impending attack and defeated a larger American army under the command of the hapless Horatio Gates. Cornwallis didn't so much win it as Gates lost it, but for the moment it looked to both sides as if the British plan to roll up the Americans from the south might work. Within earshot of the battle was the Loyalist settler Alexander Chesney, who described the totality of the British win. "On the 16th (of August, 1780) we heard heavy firing towards Camden, which kept us in the utmost anxiety untill the 18th when a letter was received from Captain Ross, aid de camp to Lord Cornwallis informing us that his Lordship had attacked & defeated Gates' Army, had killed or taken 2,200 men, 18 ammunition Waggons and 350 waggons with provisions and other stores. This news made us as happy as people in our situation could possibly be."

The Battle of Camden, South Carolina, was one of the Americans' lowest points in the war. After just an hour of fighting, the poorly led troops under General Horatio Gates turned and fled, but not fast enough to catch their commander, who was long gone by that time. Courtesy National Archives.

After the Battle of Camden, Cornwallis sent Tarleton and the Scottish light-infantry specialist Patrick Ferguson deep into the South Carolina forest to punish the rebels and recruit Loyalists. Among the Loyalists who would fall in with Ferguson was Chesney, who had been encouraged to rejoin the cause of the Crown by Clinton's successful siege of Charleston. Along for the ride was Chesney's father, who during one particularly hot skirmish found himself in the crossfire, not understanding which fire was friendly and which was not. "I placed him near a tree until the affair was over, and resolved he should not be so exposed again," Chesney wrote later.

Through the hills and hollows this rolling fight continued, neither side able to gain the upper hand. One day's battle bled into the following day's battle, with little to distinguish one day from the next. Chesney did his best to document the campaign, but the repetition got the better of him: "I was present also at a small affair at Fair Forest, the particulars of which, as well as numerous other skirmishes having escaped my memory; scarcely a day passed without some fighting."

America's Revolution, now passing its fifth year, hung in the balance in the swamps and thickets of the Carolina backcountry in desperate fights to the death not between Americans and the British, but between Americans and Americans.

South Carolina, wrote McCrady, "was to be rent and torn and trampled as no other State in the Union . . . Her people were to fall by the sword, and to be consumed by the fire; they were to be oppressed not only by the stranger, but every one by another, every one by his neighbor."

The action made and destroyed reputations. Tarleton virtually made himself mad trying to track down and capture

Francis Marion, the Swamp Fox, whose men would materialize long enough to fire a volley into British columns before evaporating into the forest. For miles and miles Tarleton chased Marion through the dank and mossy swamps to no avail, before pronouncing that the devil himself would be unable to catch the elusive patriot. Both Tarleton and Cornwallis were of the military school that liked to line up and charge, but the Swamp Fox would have none of it. Though the Swamp Fox has been deified in modern pop culture, the fact of the matter is that he and Tarleton were peas in a pod who essentially deserved each other. Indeed, Cornwallis complained bitterly of Marion's atrocities and terroristic tactics against the Loyalists, an objection that is all the more rich considering that his own subordinates were doing the exact same thing.

Part of the umbrage, of course, was that men like Marion very much saved the day for the rebellion—this despite being unpaid (the Gamecock Thomas Sumter "paid" his men in slaves captured from the Loyalists) and so poorly supplied that men sometimes went into battle unarmed, where they would wait to grab a musket from a fallen comrade.

In a sense, these South Carolina rebels were acting much like the sand and resilient palmetto logs of the fort at Sullivan's Island, absorbing blow after blow, and doing more damage to the attacker than the attacked. The more scraps that the British won, the greater their losses, first because their lost men could not be replaced, and second because their violent and heavy-handed victory dances drove more fence-sitters into the rebel camp.

Still, while the patriots were not breaking, neither were they inflicting much material damage on the British forces.

Further, if nothing else, these losses—even if just on paper—took a psychological toll, and after nearly two years of hitting and running, and the unmitigated disaster at Camden, the rebels needed something more than a moral victory.

It would be delivered to them largely by the Republic of Watauga, a curious jurisdiction of mountain men who had established an effectively autonomous government over the Eastern Continental Divide that for a time was informally known as America's fourteenth state, which went by the name of Frankland.

The Watauga lands in what is now eastern Tennessee were settled by Daniel Boone, among others, having been purchased, kinda, from the Cherokee Indians. The settlement was bolstered by refugees from the North Carolina War of Regulation in 1771, a rebellion of western settlers protesting government taxation and control. The coalition drew up its own constitution and, after being denied annexation into Virginia, washed its hands of both Crown and colonial authorities and operated as an independent government. The British naturally considered the land purchase and these "Overmountain" settlements to be illegal and ordered settlers to leave—this being the short explanation for why the Overmountain Men were so passionate for the American cause.

With renewed chestiness following the Battle of Camden in August, Ferguson—leading an army of perhaps 1,100 Americans who remained loyal to the Crown—sent a message to the Overmountain settlements demanding surrender under pain of complete annihilation. That was all it took. Unschooled in the finer arts of public relations, Ferguson's bellicose threat backfired with a roar that welled up from the rugged Appalachians. Had he thought, he might have realized that men and women who would up and form their own state would not, as a rule, accept instructions from some bossy, self-important little bird like Ferguson. Under the leadership of Isaac Shelby and John Sevier, the Overmountain settlements acted like the autonomous state they claimed to be. They manufactured their own powder and ammunition, sewed their own uniforms, and lined up financing for the expedition through a wealthy benefactor. Adding 400 of its own men to existing colonial forces, the fired-up Overmountain Men charged down out of the Appalachian highlands and into South Carolina history.

Aware by now of what he'd stirred up, Ferguson retreated and hunkered down on a bump on the landscape that bore the perhaps overreaching name of King's Mountain. On the afternoon of October 7, 1780, perhaps 1,000 patriots surrounded the mountain and charged up its slopes, shrieking in a precursor of the rebel yell. Loyalists in equal numbers beat them back, only to see the rebels regroup and charge again. The second offensive was repulsed, and the third, and so it went in fierce and desperate pulsations until the Loyalist force was diminished by sharpshooters to the point that the hill was no longer defensible. Chesney said that the Loyalists would have been able to hold the ridge, except that the wooded slopes gave the rebels their favored form of fighting—ducking behind a tree and bringing down a moving target with an almost comically long rifle. Deer or Loyalist, it was all the same to them, and they were good at it. The intense fighting lasted sixty-five minutes, and no one could argue with the bravery shown on either side.

Ferguson—who had the distinction of being the only regular soldier and, somewhat incredibly, the only non-American on the field—fell, shot through seven or eight times. When the rebels gained the higher end of the ridge and were positioned to overrun the Loyalists, white flags began to flutter.

At first it appeared that the Overmountain Men and their comrades would give no quarter, just as Tarleton's men had done—certainly the debacle at Waxhaws Creek was fresh in their mind, as men chanted Tarleton's name in the battle's final throes. A secondary problem was that the rebel forces had no true overall commander. No fewer than ten men were in charge of their various units, neither giving or taking orders from any of the others. At last, however, some of the rebel officers were able to rein in the men before things got entirely out of hand, and the patriots wound up taking 800 Loyalist prisoners.

The Battle of King's Mountain was as stunning and consequential as it was brief. It broke the back of Loyalist forces in South Carolina, and the specter of these Overmountain banshees harassing his exposed flank convinced Cornwallis to abandon his plan to invade North Carolina.

After the war, North Carolina—of which Tennessee was then a part—gave the Overmountain territory to Congress to pay off its war debt. This was to be the fourteenth state, the State of Frankland, and it was so governed for nearly five years. But due to a number of snags, only seven states voted for its admittance, two short of the two-thirds necessary under the Articles of Confederation.

Although greatly overshadowed by Trenton, Saratoga, and Yorktown, military historian John Watts De Peyster wrote that King's Mountain was "the decisive battle of the

Revolutionary War in the south, and, perhaps, the decisive result everywhere." The coup de grâce in South Carolina would be delivered at Cowpens by Nathaniel Greene and the savvy and ornery frontiersman Daniel Morgan, whose hatred for the British was born when he punched a superior officer in a 1775 campaign and was sentenced to 499 lashes, which usually spelled death.

Morgan survived and was in command of the field at Cowpens on January 17, 1781, where he had the pleasure of giving Tarleton his comeuppance. In fact, Morgan tricked both the British and his own forces, which included a significant number of South Carolina militia. Aware of the militia's habit of disappearing into the swamps shortly after a battle had been joined, Morgan made sure a river was at his army's back to prevent premature flight. He then baited Tarleton into the open ground the officer, like all British, so greatly coveted in battle.

Morgan turned his militia into thespians, instructing them to fire twice, then turn to the left and run. Behind the militia, however, were two more lines of increasingly better Continental troops. Salivating over a clean shot at the enemy, Tarleton's aggression played perfectly into Morgan's hands. When the militia fled, Tarleton misconstrued the scene as total victory, and wound up charging straight into the guns of Morgan's best soldiers. When the confused British turned away to escape, they found themselves facing the American militia, which had come full circle around the back of the American lines and reformed. Many British soldiers were so confused they dropped to the ground, whether they had been shot or not. It was a complete physical and psychological beating.

Morgan's tactics went down not only as the most innovative of the entire Revolution, but as one of the more successful battle plans in all of American military history.

The war in the Carolina swamps was now over. Greene chased Cornwallis up to Yorktown, where nine months later the British commander surrendered. History would record that although the British lost the war in Virginia, they were beaten in South Carolina.

Chapter 10

Celebrating a Stalemate

General William Howe knew how to make an exit, and by the spring of 1778 he was ready to make one. There were plenty of those willing to help him along, of course, mostly in the form of impatient Parliament members who were frustrated at Howe's blasé attitude toward quelling the rebellion.

It was true that Howe had technically won the battle of Bunker Hill (at the cost of more than 1,000 casualties, more than the British would lose in any other battle for the remainder of the war) and captured the important American cities of New York and Philadelphia. But he also appeared to be dragging his feet every step of the way, which led some to whisper that he had patriotic tendencies. However that might have been, the more believable explanation is that he was too attached to his creature comforts, and the creature he was comfortable with at the moment was the blonde Boston bombshell, twenty-five-year-old Elizabeth Lloyd Loring. It is impossible to find a description of Loring that does not begin with the words "generously endowed," and this, or these, was only the beginning of her charms.

Loring, or "the Sultana" as she was widely known, was the star of the Boston social pages by day, while the night would find her drinking many a man under the table and staying up late in the gambling halls.

In a deliciously saucy book, *The Making of the Prefident 1789: The Unauthorized Campaign Biography*, Marvin Kitman wrote, "Elizabeth Lloyd Loring on her back did more than most daughters of the Revolution did standing up," and quotes a popular poem of the day by Francis Hopkinson:

> *Sir William he, snug as a flea,*
> *Lay all this time a snoring.*
> *Nor dreamed of harm as he lay warm,*
> *In bed with Mrs. Loring.*

This was one of the cleaner ditties at the time—others related to the grabbing of Howe's "warlike staff." As for the suggestion that Betsy was a closet patriot, it's hard to tell. Patriots had burned her country home, causing her to flee to the safety of Boston, so there wouldn't seem to have been any love lost, but motivations and intrigue ran so deep in those days anything was possible.

Mr. Loring, whose first name was Joshua, had no particular objection to the relationship, since he'd been given the plum job of selling food to British prisons that held rebel prisoners. Mr. Loring took the money and returned little in the way of sustenance, making him widely regarded as a heartless bastard. In that time and place, he would not have particularly stood out.

While in New York, Howe's eye wandered to another woman of distinction, Judith Verplanck, the wife and business partner of Samuel Verplanck. Samuel was a patriot, Judith a Loyalist, an inconvenience they worked around by temporarily splitting up—Judith stayed in the British-controlled city while Samuel retreated to an estate in the countryside. Judith entertained Howe, and although the seriousness of their relationship is unknown, Howe was happy in the company of both Betsy and Judith, with Joshua Loring in the background, contentedly gambling away the proceeds awarded him by the British government. It was quite the arrangement, and one that Howe clearly preferred to actual battle. (The patriots had their paramours as well, a passel whom Kitman refers to as the Founding Girlfriends; writing for the *Huffington Post,* he says he has found "at least nine women who could have said in all honesty George Washington slept here.")

Intentional or not, Betsy had one more contribution to make to the Patriot cause. Howe had dutifully taken her and her husband to New York under roughly the same arrangement as in Boston, and on Howe's curiously circuitous route from New York to Philadelphia, Betsy gets the credit/blame for insisting on an ocean rather than an overland passage. (Some of the Loring legend is almost assuredly contrived, the product, more than one researcher has suggested, of historians' overstimulated imaginations.) Whatever the reason, the roundabout and the time it took to negotiate it were costly.

Howe's army took Philadelphia easily enough, but lacked time to further damage Washington's army before winter set in. This was somewhat typical of the jousting between Washington and Howe in the early part of the war, with the British winning battles but losing the advantage. One foreign officer quipped to Washington, "You have conquered General Howe, but his troops have beaten yours." Howe's decision to winter in Philadelphia allowed Washington's men to live to fight another day; granted, they lived miserably through the storied winter at Valley Forge, but survived as a fighting force nonetheless.

Howe's venture south also left the British army to the north high and dry, where—without reinforcements from Howe—it eventually lost to the Americans at Saratoga. Largely because of this defeat, it was felt in British circles that Howe needed to be replaced, a theory that had no greater advocate than Howe himself.

With one foot all but out the door, Howe had no interest in taking the fight to General Washington's shivering troops in Valley Forge. The Continental Army held a strong defensive position, but had little else going for it, as through the brutal winter 2,500 men died of malnutrition, disease, and exposure.

Twenty miles to the south, the British were in a far more enviable position, even if rebel raiders made supplying the city problematic. Jefferson preferred the look of Philadelphia to

London and even Paris. It was a city of 30,000 residents, many of whom were Quakers who had accumulated some degree of wealth, but, wrote Winthrop Sargent, "by religion (were) averse to the gayeties of life." The Quakers were allowed to eat, however, and "being the only carnal vanity that it was lawful for a Quaker to indulge in," the city was famous for its exquisite tables. The dress might have been a little behind the latest fashion in England, but the conversation was witty and well-informed, the art was sophisticated and the women, according to Abigail Adams, represented a "constellation of beauties." For Howe, it would do.

The winter passed with balls, banquets, theatrical productions, and high-stakes card games that wiped out the savings of more than a few British officers. Howe had tendered his resignation in October 1777, but it wasn't until April 1788 that he received word that it had been accepted.

Pending his departure, his men decided to throw him a party, and for organizing the affair they turned to John André. Everyone, even George Washington, was sad to see André hanged two years later for turning Benedict Arnold. It seemed in some circles that perhaps it would be enough to just give André a good talking to, but of course that would not have been acceptable.

But the spring of 1778 was a happier time for everyone except the Quakers, who watched the British party animals with disgust. André was just the man to put the exclamation point on Howe's American career. Save for perhaps General John Burgoyne, André was unmatched for his charm, sophistication, and abilities in writing, theater and, the arts. He would not be content to throw a mere party, and indeed a new word, Mischianza, was coined out of the Italian word for "a little of this and a little of that." Except that it would not be a little, it would be a lot. "Nothing like it, either before or since," wrote eighteenth-century Philadelphia historian Howard Malcom Jenkins, "ever disgraced the army of a great nation."

Vegas only wished it could put on a party like the irrepressible John André, who attended to every detail, from making costumes to painting the banquet hall. Tickets were engraved with a wreath-bound shield depicting the sun setting on the ocean surrounded with various military accoutrements and a banner with the Latin words *Lucco discedens, aucto splendore resurgam*, which translated to "I descend in light, and shall rise again in splendor." André was never accused of understatement.

The Mischianza began in the morning of May 18, 1778, on the Delaware River with a procession of ships, galleys, and flatboats, gaily upholstered with carpets, banners, and pennants, carrying all the shining lights of the British army, including, of course, Howe himself. To the thunder of guns from the British warships, these luminaries were deposited south of the city on a grand, grassy promenade where they made their way to pavilions from which to view the afternoon entertainment. Ladies decked out in Turkish garb arrived through a triumphal arch and were seated at the fore of the pavilions, where knights arrived to flourish of trumpets.

Among the Ladies of the Burning Mountain, whose honor was fought over in a celebratory mock joust, was Peggy Shippen, who would become the second wife of Benedict Arnold and an influence in his decision to cast his allegiance with the British. Courtesy National Archives.

Once they were in place, a herald (with a backdrop of more trumpets) proclaimed "The knights of the Blended Rose, by me their herald, proclaim and assert that the ladies of the

Blended Rose excel in wit, beauty, and every accomplishment, those of the whole world; and should any knight or knights be so hardy as to dispute or deny it, they are ready to enter the list with them, and maintain their assertions by deeds of arms, according to the laws of ancient chivalry."

Well, if there were any other knights within hearing distance, they were not likely to stand for this, and sure enough, as luck would have it another herald rode from beneath the arch with the rejoinder: "The knights of the Burning Mountain present themselves here, not to contest by words, but to disprove by deeds, the vainglorious assertion of the knights of the Blended Rose, and enter these lists to maintain that the ladies of the Burning Mountain are not excelled in beauty, virtue, or accomplishments by any in the universe," etc.

This was strong stuff, and there would no doubt be blood, but first the knights spent considerable time pledging their devotion to the turban-headed ladies and promising them that their honor would be classically defended. This they did, charging back and forth with lances piercing, swords waving, and pistols firing until the field marshal raced in and assured one and all that the fair damsels were quite convinced of their bravery, allowing the Knights of the Blended Rose and Burning Mountain to quit the field with honor, their robes a-flowing and silks a-fluttering as military bands blared their salutations.

One and all then repaired to the estate's mansion, which had been decorated with murals, flowers and, for effect, eighty-five mirrors. The party enjoyed snacks and libations and danced until 10:00 that night, when the windows were cast open and a bouquet of rockets exploded to announce the coming of a long and elaborate fireworks. The pyrotechnics went on until midnight, when dinner was served in a specially built dining hall more than 200 feet in length, its decor best explained by Andre himself:

"The ceiling was the segment of a circle, and the sides were painted of a light straw color, with vine leaves and festoons of flowers, some in a bright, some in a darkish green. Fifty-six large pier-glasses, ornamented with green silk artificial flowers and ribbons; one hundred branches, with three lights in each, trimmed in the same manner as the mirrors; eighteen lusters, each with twenty-four lights, suspended from the ceiling, and ornamented as the branches; three hundred wax tapers, disposed along the supper-tables; four hundred and thirty covers; twelve hundred dishes; twenty-four black slaves in Oriental dresses, with silver collars and bracelets, ranged in two lines, and bending to the ground as the general and admiral approached the saloon; all these, forming together the most brilliant assemblage of gay objects, and appearing at once as we entered by an easy descent, exhibited a *coup d'œil* beyond description magnificent."

If the Quakers hadn't been ready for the British to leave before, they were now. The Quaker diarist Elizabeth Drinker wrote sternly, "On ye river Sky-Rockets and other Fire Works were exhibited after night. How insensible do these people appear, while our Land is so greatly desolated, and Death and sore destruction has overtaken, and now descends over so many." After dinner, the dancing resumed and lasted until 4:00 in the morning. So grand and splendid was Howe's send-off that the casual viewer might have wondered what would have happened if the general had actually won.

CHAPTER 11

Stories Best Forgotten

As Howe demonstrated, some of the best military histo-
ries are born out of defeat. And through the course of
the war, the Americans perhaps suffered no greater defeat than
they did in a picturesque, island-studded bay in Down East
Maine at the mouth of the Penobscot River.

By 1779, much of the war's focus had turned to the South,
where the British had captured Savannah and had set their
sight on the Carolinas. Wanting a more secure toehold in the
North, however, they looked to a strategic stretch of coastline in Massachusetts (now Maine) that would serve as a base
for attacking American privateers and as a home for displaced
Loyalists.

The colony was to be called New Ireland, and 700 soldiers
were ordered to inhabit the upper portion of Penobscot Bay
and build a defensive works that would come to be known

as Fort George. Legendary explorers Samuel de Champlain and John Smith had come within a year or two of bumping into each other there in the early 1600s, and the English and French had spent the next century and a half squabbling over the territory, which was important for furs, fish, and timber. The Dutch got in on the action too, and American colonists helped themselves to the coastline after the French were evicted from North America following the Seven Years' War.

So there was a great deal of harrumphing in Boston when word arrived that the British had swarmed in and seized the village of Castine. The Americans were determined to do something about this atrocity, and they were not inclined to employ half measures. It might have appeared that they were using a Howitzer to go after a hen, but no matter: Massachusetts authorized an $8 million expedition that included forty-four ships, 1,000 marines and militia under the command respectively of Commodore Dudley Saltonstall and Brigadier General Solomon Lovell, and a 100-man artillery force led by none other than Paul Revere. The expedition sailed on July 19, intent on making mincemeat of the tiny enemy outpost, an outcome that was assumed not just by the Americans, but by the British themselves. When he saw the considerable American fleet entering the bay, the bemused British commander General Francis McLean would later remark that he had intended to fire off a couple rounds for form's sake and then surrender. Instead, he had a front-row seat to an American naval debacle the likes of which would not be seen again until Pearl Harbor.

From the beginning, the Americans seemed timid, aborting offensives after the loss of the first man. On July 28, Brigadier General Peleg Wadsworth led 400 marines and militia to capture the heights leading to the fort, but the initiative was lost when Saltonstall refused to offer the ground force the cover of his considerable fleet. For two weeks, Lovell begged Saltonstall for help. For two weeks, Saltonstall danced just out of range of the British guns, while failing to allow the American ground force to advance. When Saltonstall finally did decide to join the fray, it could hardly have come at a worse time.

The beleaguered Fort George had gotten word of its predicament to Captain George Collier, who arrived in Penobscot Bay with ten warships just as Saltonstall entered the mouth of the Penobscot River. Saltonstall realized too late that he had nowhere to go. Collier chased his fleet up the Penobscot to the falls at present-day Bangor, picking off the American ships one by one. Realizing their condition was hopeless, American sailors abandoned their ships and set them afire to keep them out of British hands.

Of the forty-four ships that had set out from Boston less than a month prior, only one remained afloat, after it was captured. Having lost their ride home, the Americans were forced to find their way overland back to Boston, a distance of nearly 250 miles. Far more men were lost in this difficult retreat than in the assault itself.

The blame for the epic failure fell largely on the shoulders of Saltonstall, who was court-martialed. Found guilty, he was dismissed from military service. Also accused of cowardice and disobedience was Paul Revere. Revere—who said his accusers bore him ill based on long-standing grudges—wrote a passionate defense of his actions and begged for his day in court. Out of the entire expedition, only Peleg Wadsworth, who has since been largely forgotten by history, distinguished himself both for being about the only American officer to take the offensive during the attack, and for effectively organizing the overland march through the Maine wilderness back home to Boston.

Paul Revere was court-martialed and cleared of the charges brought against him. Although he was not disciplined, neither was he celebrated; since Revere was only one among perhaps twenty riders who had helped spread the word of the British advance five years earlier, there was no real thought of his being a hero at the time. Nor would he be known today, had not, eighty years later, Peleg Wadsworth's grandson Henry not picked up a pen and written the immortal lines that begin, "Listen my children and you shall hear . . ."

As with Revere, just as the winning side gets to choose its heroes, it also gets to overlook its goats. An early candidate in the war would have been General Adam Stephen, a Virginian who wanted to be like Washington, but just wasn't made of the same stuff.

On the day after Christmas, 1776, it was Washington, however, who needed a spot of good luck. The year had been miserable, as the Continental Army had been pushed out of New York and across New Jersey, and even Washington himself believed the end was nigh. He had one last plan, though: to cross the Delaware River and shock 1,400 Hessians at Trenton who, it might be hoped, would have their guard down because of the holiday. Secrecy, obviously, was paramount for the mission to succeed.

The mission, however, was not secret; very few secrets ever were, since the combatants were so much cut of the same cloth. Tories and British spies visited the Hessian camp in the days leading up to Christmas with news of an American attack. Nor was the crossing of the Delaware and subsequent march to Trenton a picnic for the Americans, with terrible weather forcing the plot to fall further behind schedule. Washington's men were clothed in rags, the gunpowder was getting wet, and the snow was reddened with the blood of the army's shoeless feet. Suddenly and without warning, the Continental Army was startled by the appearance of fifty armed men approaching on the road from Trenton. They were more startled to find out that the band comprised American soldiers who had crossed the river on their own to avenge the Hessians' killing of one of their brethren.

Washington was beyond furious. All the meticulous time and attention to detail he had spent in advance of this one last chance to save the patriot cause had in all likelihood been compromised by a Continental hothead (not that this was a scarce breed of cat). Storming through the company to find the miscreant responsible for this harebrained idea, he heard a name that made his skin crawl: Brigadier General Adam Stephen.

He might have known. For more than a decade this Scottish-born physician, speculator, and scoundrel-in-residence with a reputation for vice and thuggery had dogged Washington on the Virginia frontier, meddling in his business plans and running (unsuccessfully) against him for office. Washington froze in rage when he caught sight of Stephen: "*You*! You sir may have ruined all my plans by having put them on their guard." And that was just the beginning. Washington had a temper, but onlookers agreed later that this outburst had topped the previous record.

Stephen, for his part, had only been acting in the typical manner of the frontier, and no doubt regarded Washington as some sort of patriotic drama king in sore need of lightening up. As it turned out, Stephen might actually have done his adversary a favor. Having been warned repeatedly of an imminent American attack, the Hessians most likely thought Stephen's careless advance was it, and had settled back with some relief that it was over.

Nine months later, Stephen was in hot water again, but this time the consequences, both to him and to the Continental Army, were more severe. General Howe had just whipped Washington at the Battle of Brandywine on September 11, 1777, badly schooling the American general on the art of military maneuvering and allowing the British to take the city of Philadelphia. It was a tenuous occupation. Patriots had destroyed storehouses and booby-trapped the Delaware River. Howe, whose ships, laden with food and armaments, were still at sea, was forced to extend himself dangerously far from his base to attack American outposts that were in position to disrupt British supply lines.

With the British army split between Philadelphia and Germantown, a century-old, stone-house settlement six miles northwest of the city, Washington saw an excellent chance to even the score and, with a little luck, retake the city. On October 4, Washington swept down on Germantown from the north, aiming the main body of his army at the British center while wheeling three columns around to the east to attack the British right. Ominously, one of these columns was under the command of Adam Stephen.

The Battle of Germantown began at 5:00 in the morning, but the sixteen-mile night march that preceded it gave Stephen a chance to get good and drunk before his men entered the fray. So he was in fine fighting trim by the time he split off from the main body of the army as part of the flanking maneuver led by General Nathaniel Greene.

George Washington was often frustrated by unprofessional underlings. At the Battle of Germantown, his daring plan to oust the British from Philadelphia was done in by the fog and an officer, Adam Stephen, who was in a fog of his own. Courtesy National Archives.

The light was dim and a thick fog was rolling over the landscape, so perhaps the fact that Stephen was hammered had nothing to do with it. But his brigade became separated from Greene's force and Stephen went trundling down the wrong road, which more or less marked the end of Washington's planned pincer movement.

Despite a few early hiccups, the Americans had a chance, perhaps even a good one. The main American force under

General John Sullivan ran into the British outside the town and opened fire. Unable to be certain what they were up against, British officers assumed that an American scouting party had stumbled upon their ranks and ordered their men to make rebel stew out of the stray outfit.

The redcoats formed up and sent a fierce volley into the fog, a demonstration that was returned in kind. Quizzically, they turned to look at their commanders. Something wasn't right. Howe himself rode to the fore and chided his light infantry for its failure to advance. He was practically in mid-sentence when the American artillery thundered to life. The British fell back and then made a tough defensive stand in the face of the American onslaught. If the Americans executed everything perfectly, Howe might crack and withdraw down the Delaware, leaving the Continental Army to spend a cozy winter in Philadelphia. If they didn't, it was cold, barren Valley Forge for them.

As the battle hung in the balance, Stephen persevered and soon ran into a brigade of roughly the same strength under the command of General Anthony Wayne. Stephen's troops valiantly tore into the opposing force, which might have been considered heroic, except of course that Wayne and Stephen were supposed to be fighting on the same side.

Wayne was stunned. The fog-cloaked attack was coming from a direction that made no sense. "Mad Anthony" never dreamed that he could be under attack from his compatriots, so he assumed that the wily British had maneuvered into a position on his flank. His men leveled their guns in Stephen's direction. Heavy casualties mounted on both sides until each simultaneously considered itself defeated and turned and fled into adjoining American units, causing mass confusion. Whatever shot Washington's army might have had was gone. Too much had gone wrong, and the British had been too good. The best the Americans could salvage was the genuine sense that they had gone toe-to-toe with the enemy and lost only because the breaks hadn't fallen their way. A court-martial quickly determined Stephen's condition and culpability, and he was dismissed from service. He returned to his rural Virginia home and prepared for the next phase of his life as a city planner.

Where Stephen's luck had been bad, General Horatio Gates was blessed with a turn of events that even the best of novelists couldn't have constructed. A competent administrator with valuable prior experience in the British army, Gates dreamed of battlefield heroics, much as the backup quarterback dreams of doing more than carrying the clipboard.

Politically astute, Gates fanned anti-Washington flames in Congress, and seems to have participated in a borderline conspiracy to oust his commanding officer and take over the army himself. Seldom a fan of offensive warfare, Gates could always be counted on in councils of war to vote for falling back instead of going on the attack, to the point that James Madison referred to Gates and his cronies as "the honorable society of midwives."

As Washington's reputation slumped in the waning months of 1776, Gates thought he had spotted his chance to take his case to Congress when Washington—foolishly, Gates thought—hatched a cockamamie scheme to paddle across the icy Delaware River over the Christmas holidays and take on a force of tough Hessian soldiers at Trenton. As Washington made preparations, Gates faked illness and then traveled to Baltimore, where Congress was meeting. Gates planned to be front and center as an able replacement when news arrived of Washington's inevitable and ignominious defeat. When it didn't work out that way, Gates not only failed in the "I told you so" department, he also failed to be part of the battle where he might have accumulated a little reflected glory.

He would, however, be at Saratoga, New York, to accept the surrender of British General John Burgoyne after a spirited battle that he had little to do with. Today he is still widely known as the hero of Saratoga, even though he was in effect dragged to victory kicking and screaming by the battle's real heroes. These included Benedict Arnold and the rawboned frontiersman Daniel Morgan, perhaps the war's most under-rated officer. Defying Gates's orders, Arnold rode into battle and led the Americans in the day's decisive action.

In artist John Trumbull's classic painting *Surrender of General Burgoyne,* Benedict Arnold is nowhere to be seen, disgraced by this point as a turncoat. Instead, a heroic and magnanimous Horatio Gates dominates the scene, conqueror by default. He parlayed Saratoga into an appointment to the southern command, where once again he found himself in the center of a critical battle. Only this time, there was no Benedict Arnold to bail him out.

Historians have many words for Gates's performance at the important crossroads of Camden, South Carolina, in 1780, but "humiliating" seems to be the one of which they are most fond. Left to his own designs, without the savvy second tier of officers he enjoyed at Saratoga, Gates blundered badly, mismatching his flighty militia against tough British regulars, while sending his own best men against British-army afterthoughts. It was over in an hour, but Gates didn't even make it that long. He fled along with the greenest militia, which, if one is searching for bright sides, abandoned the field so fast that virtually nobody got hurt. Gates, for his part, appropriated what was by consensus viewed as the finest racehorse in the vicinity and spurred it to the north, not stopping until he was in Charlotte, North Carolina, some sixty miles away. He would never fight again.

Gates, in the final analysis, shared many similarities with another British veteran, General Charles Lee, who, according to General Charles Lee, was the greatest commander the Americans had and their only chance at victory. Lee's former experience in the British Army was assumed to count for something until events proved otherwise. Also like Gates, Lee felt he should have Washington's job, and if he had spent half as much energy planning to overthrow the British as he spent plotting to overthrow Washington, the war could have been over in a few months.

Lee might have been a somewhat better officer than Gates or Stephen, but his reputation had been burnished as well by a victory not of his own doing. In the British Army's first attempt to take Charleston in 1776, Lee ordered the South Carolinians to fall back into a defensive position. Retreat was not what the city defenders had in mind, so they simply ignored the Yankee officer and proceeded to drive the British back out to sea. Up north, however, these details escaped notice, and Lee was hailed as a hero.

Lee in truth was no better at taking orders himself, especially from General George Washington, whom he viewed with disdain. Later in 1776, as Washington was retreating from

New York and New Jersey into Pennsylvania, Lee disregarded orders and dragged his feet, largely because he was spending most of his time writing to representatives in Congress urging them to put him in charge.

"(H)ad I the powers I could do you much good, might I but dictate one week," Lee wrote to Benjamin Rush. Lee complained about Washington's indecision, while at the same time failing to respond to direct orders demanding haste. Lee's simultaneous sabotage of Washington's wishes and PR campaign in Congress appeared to be working; members of Congress wrote Lee glowing letters, and Washington might have been one misstep away from a shift in power when fate stepped in and said, "enough."

In his 1858 work *The Treason of Charles Lee*, New York Historical Society Librarian George Henry Moore credited Lee's "insatiable ambition and ungovernable selfishness" for what happened next. At noon on Friday, December 13, Lee and a small detail were dawdling at White's Tavern, at what he thought was a safe distance from the British advance through New Jersey. However, on a reconnaissance mission, Banastre Tarleton and the King's Dragoon Guards got wind of Lee's location from a Tory who was disgruntled with Lee's men for taking his horse. After a brief resistance, Moore wrote that Lee "fell upon his knees . . . and all agree that he behaved in a most cowardly manner, apparently frantic with terror and disappointment." In captivity, Lee did little to polish his reputation. He babbled on to the British about the weakness of the American army, assuring them that "The game is nearly at an end."

Still, Lee's reputation was such that his capture caused dejection in the American ranks and great celebration among the British, who felt that America could not stand the loss of he whom they considered to be its best general. That assumption was almost immediately reconsidered with Washington's victories at Trenton and Princeton to close out the year. Nor was public reaction on both sides of the ocean shared by those who knew Lee best. Sir Joseph Yorke, a British minister at the Hague, wrote that he hoped Lee would be returned to the Americans soon because "he was the worst present that could be made to any army."

Shockingly, in the hope of saving his own skin, Lee wrote a lengthy white paper for the British, detailing how best to defeat the American army. This, Moore wrote, "vindicate(d) his claim to a high place upon that list of traitors of whom . . . Judas was not the first, nor Benedict Arnold the last." If the British were grateful for the intelligence, they didn't show it. In the spring of 1778 they were more than happy to exchange Lee for one of their own, and let the Americans deal with him.

Lee was in trouble again barely a month later, this time at the Battle of Monmouth, where he was ordered to lead a frontal assault against the British. Instead, Lee retreated, right into the arms of George Washington and his advancing soldiers. Once again, the commander's legendary temper erupted at the insubordination much as it had against Adam Stephen two years prior. Lee responded in kind, but this time his disrespect of Washington cost him. In July he was court-martialed and convicted of disobedience, misbehavior, and disrespect, and released from duty.

Lee, Gates, and Stephen, this rogue's gallery of American generals, had one more thing in common. All retired to estates that joined in what is now West Virginia's Eastern Panhandle. Gates built a home called Travelers Rest on his 660-acre plantation (he sold the estate in 1790, freed his slaves, and moved to New York). Four miles away, Leetown is named for Charles. Stephen built a hunting lodge a mile away on the Opequon Creek and laid out plans for present-day Martinsburg. The town was named after Stephen's friend, Colonel Thomas Martin, who returned the favor by founding Stephens City, Virginia, thirty miles to the south. In the West Virginia Panhandle, at least, the generals' sins are today forgiven and their positive points remembered. All three of their houses still stand.

All took their forced retirements in relatively good humor. They gathered often, usually at Lee's home, where the "wine flowed freely" to recount past exploits, Lee of course being the one who needed to have the last word. On one such night, Lee raised his glass and said, "The county of Berkeley is indeed to be congratulated. You, Stephen, distinguished yourself by getting drunk when you should have remained sober; you, Gates, were cashiered for retreating when you should have been advancing, while your humble servant covered himself with glory and laurels and was cashiered for advancing when he should have been retreating."

The war over, everyone was free to laugh.

Selected titles for further reading

Memorial of Enoch Brown and Eleven Scholars Who Were Massacred in Antrim Township, Franklin County, Pennsylvania, by the Indians During the Pontiac War, July 26, 1764, edited by the Reverend Cyrus Cort. 1886, free ebook available.

Never Come to Peace Again; Pontiac's Uprising and the Fate of the British Empire in North America, by David Dixon, University of Oklahoma Press, 2005.

Biography of Captain Charles Grant, 42nd or Royal Highland Regiment, by Paul Pace, online, smithrebellion1765.com.

A Struggle for Power: The American Revolution, by Theodore Draper, Random House, 1996.

The Black Boys Uprising of 1765: Traders, Troops and "Rioters" during Pontiac's War, by Dan Guzy, The Conococheague Institute, 2014.

Colonel James Smith's Life Among the Delawares, 1755–1759, a first-hand account of eighteenth-century Indian life in Smith's four years of captivity. Edited by Horace Kephart, Outing Publishing, New York, 1915. Smith's account of his life in captivity is largely beyond the scope of this book, but is fascinating in its own right.

Narrative of Colonel Ethan Allen's Captivity, by Ethan Allen, Fourth Edition, with notes, Burlington: Chauncey Goodrich, 1846.

Ethan Allen: His Life and Times, by Willard Sterne Randall, W.W. Norton, 2011.

General Orders of Geo. Washington, Commander-in-chief of the Army of the Revolution, Issued at Newburgh on the Hudson, 1782–1783.

The Life of Benedict Arnold: His Patriotism and His Treason, by Isaac Newton Arnold, Jansen, McClurg & Co., 1880. (Note: Isaac Arnold came from the New England family of Benedict Arnold, and was perhaps Benedict's first defender. Isaac does not deny the crime, but attempts to place it in proper context. In the twenty-first century, more historians have examined Benedict Arnold's feats of courage and heroism as well as his defection.)

History of Norwich, Connecticutt: From Its Possession by the Indians to the Year 1866, by Frances Manwaring Caulkins, H.P. Haven, 1874, free ebook available.

The Letters of John and Abigail Adams, by John Adams, Abigail Adams.

Pox Americana: The Great Smallpox Epidemic of 1775–82, by Elizabeth Fenn, Hill and Wang, New York, 2001.

"Smallpox," George Washington's Mount Vernon, online, mountvernon.org.

Cotton Mather and Salem Witchcraft, by William Frederick Poole, University Press: Welch, Bigelow, & Co., 1869, free ebook available.

The Revolutionary Adventures of Ebenezer Fox, by Ebenezer Fox, Munroe & Francis, Boston, 1838. Available as a free ebook.

The Adventures of Christopher Hawkins, by Christopher Hawkins, privately published, New York, 1864. Available as a free ebook.

Joshua Barney: Hero of the Revolution and 1812, by Louis Arthur Norton, Naval Institute Press, Annapolis Maryland, 2000.

A Biographical Memoir of the Late Commodore Joshua Barney, by Mary Barney, Gray and Bowen, Boston, 1832.

Martyrs to the Revolution in the British Prison Ships, by George Taylor, W.H. Arthur & Co. New York, 1855. Available as a free ebook.

Beaumarchais and the American Revolution, by Brian N. Morton and Donald C. Spinellu, Lexington Books, 2003.

Beaumarchais, a Biography, by Maurice Lever, Farrar, Straus and Giroux, 2009.

Memoirs of the Duc de Lauzun, Translated by E. Jules Méras, Sturgis & Walton Company, 1812.

The Campaign that won America; The Story of Yorktown, by Burke Davis, The Dial Press, 1970.

The Story of Old Fort Johnson, by W. Max Reid, online at montgomery.nygenweb.net/johnson/Chap08.html.

History of the Religious Society of Friends, Called by Some the Free Quakers in the City of Philadelphia, by Charles Wetherill, online at qhpress.org/quakerpages/qwhp/freequakers02.htm.

Haym Salomon: The Financier of the Revolution : an Unwritten Chapter in American History, by Madison Clinton Peters, Trow Press, 1911.

Intelligence in the War of Independence, publication of the Central Intelligence Agency, online at cia.gov/library/publications/intelligence-history/intelligence/intro.html, 2007.

Notable American Women, 1607–1950: A Biographical Dictionary, edited by Edward T. James, Janet Wilson James, Paul S. Boyer, Radcliffe College, 1971.

The Making of the Prefident: The Unauthorized Campaign Biography, by Marvin Kitman, Grove Press, 1989.

The Mischianza, Oatmeal for the Foxhounds, Banastre Tarleton and the British Legion, online, home.golden.net/~marg/bansite/_entry.html

American Prisoners of the Revolution, by Danske Dandridge, The Michie Company, Printers, Charlottesville, Virginia, 1911.

Memorial History of the City of Philadelphia: Special and Biographical, by Howard Malcolm Jenkins, George Overcash Seilhamer, New York History Company, New York, 1893, free ebook available.

South Carolina and the American Revolution: A Battlefield History, by John W. Gordon, University of South Carolina, 2003.

Washington's Crossing, by David Hackett Fischer, Oxford University Press, 2004.

The Buried Past: An Archaeological History of Philadelphia, by John L. Cotter, Daniel G. Roberts, and Michael Parrington, University of Pennsylvania Press, 1992.

History of Berkeley County West Virginia, by Willis F. Evans 1928, Facsimile Reprint by Heritage Books Inc., 2001.